# The Thinking Human's Guide to Religion

A Modern Interpretation of an Ancient Text

Steve Paull

Copyright © 2018 Steve Paull

ISBN: 978-1-925681-42-0
Published by Vivid Publishing
A division of Fontaine Publishing Group
P.O. Box 948, Fremantle
Western Australia 6959
www.vividpublishing.com.au

Cataloguing-in-Publication data is available from the National Library of Australia

All rights reserved. No part of this publication may be reproduced, stored in a retrieval system or transmitted in any form or by any means, electronic, mechanical, photocopying, recording or otherwise, without the prior written permission of the copyright holder. The information, views, opinions and visuals expressed in this publication are solely those of the author and do not necessarily reflect those of the publisher. The publisher disclaims any liabilities or responsibilities whatsoever for any damages, libel or liabilities arising directly or indirectly from the contents of this publication.

*Dedicated to my wife Sue, who puts up with way too much of my bullshit.*

## CONTENTS

Foreword .................................................... 6
Genesis 1 ................................................. 12
Genesis 2 ................................................. 21
Genesis 3 ................................................. 33
Genesis 4 ................................................. 38
Genesis 5 ................................................. 43
Genesis 6 ................................................. 47
Genesis 7 ................................................. 57
Genesis 8 ................................................. 66
Genesis 9 ................................................. 76
Genesis 10 ............................................... 81
Genesis 11 ............................................... 83
Genesis 12 ............................................... 89
Genesis 13 ............................................... 93
Genesis 14 ............................................... 95
Genesis 15 .............................................. 100
Genesis 16 .............................................. 107
Genesis 17 .............................................. 112
Genesis 18 .............................................. 118
Genesis 19 .............................................. 122
Genesis 20 .............................................. 130
Genesis 21 .............................................. 132
Genesis 22 .............................................. 136
Genesis 23 .............................................. 141
Genesis 24 .............................................. 143
Genesis 25 .............................................. 149
Genesis 26 .............................................. 152
Genesis 27 .............................................. 155
Genesis 28 .............................................. 159
Genesis 29 .............................................. 163

| | |
|---|---|
| Genesis 30 | 166 |
| Genesis 31 | 173 |
| Genesis 32 | 177 |
| Genesis 33 | 180 |
| Genesis 34 | 183 |
| Genesis 35 | 187 |
| Genesis 36 | 192 |
| Genesis 37 | 193 |
| Genesis 38 | 199 |
| Genesis 39 | 208 |
| Genesis 40 | 212 |
| Genesis 41 | 216 |
| Genesis 42 | 221 |
| Genesis 43 | 227 |
| Genesis 44 | 230 |
| Genesis 45 | 233 |
| Genesis 46 | 235 |
| Genesis 47 | 238 |
| Genesis 48 | 243 |
| Genesis 49 | 247 |
| Genesis 50 | 253 |
| Genesis: The Summary | 259 |
| Conclusion | 263 |

## Foreword

Hello. I'm Steve, and I rather dislike religion. No, it doesn't matter which one.

Perhaps I should explain that a little better. I'm not against, nor do I judge (well, not overly!) those people who believe in God. I just get a little disappointed that, for the few thousand years that organized religion has been in existence, people aren't more intelligent by now. We are certainly cynical enough to spot a con-job when we see one; a glance on our social media pages and emails on any given day is enough to see the myriad windfalls from Nigerian princes bequeathing two million dollars to YOU, and that all you need to do is send them $25,000 for "legal fees" and other bribes to make that money legally yours. Unfortunately though, we see almost as many people on shows like Dr. Phil who are so gullible that they have given everything but the shirt on their back, as these catfish reel them in hook, line and sinker. It really does my head in, because surely people cannot be THAT gullible, right? Any rational-thinking individual should be able to spot a con-job a mile away, and yet... and yet, millions of people are led down the primrose path by the biggest con-job the world has ever seen: religion.

The reason why, of course, is obvious. In an uncertain world, people strive to look for meaning beyond the humdrum of their daily lives. We want some assurance that our experiences and efforts have not been for nothing when we shuck our mortal coils. For some, there is a measure of comfort gleaned from the stories contained in the bible, and the promises of paradise everlasting if you live a virtuous life. For many others, the bible has become a book of moral lessons (much like Aesop's Fables), where the story is not as important as the message behind it. There are also, sadly, those select few souls who interpret the bible literally, believing everything written therein without question, considering the stories as actual recorded history, despite the glaring contradictions and overwhelming evidence to the contrary.

There is also the fear factor, fed to us from an early age to ensure our capitulation to authority by threatening us with a fiery, burning, painful eternal afterlife if we don't play nice. And so because of our instinctive aversion to pain of any kind (particularly the never-ending variety), a large percentage of the earth's population are still under the sway of a book written a few thousand years ago at best, designed to control the populace through fear. It's a sad indictment on the human race and its alleged intelligence, especially when we have achieved so much in the fields of science and technology, to help us better understand the universe we live in.

It may seem at this stage that I'm just a typical religion-bashing atheist, but that would be an unfair assessment. I lean toward the possibility that there IS some sort of existence after death; whether that be heaven or hell, limbo, purgatory, reincarnation, rattling some chains in a haunted house, evolution into a higher level of existence, or even being absorbed into some sort of universal consciousness, is up for debate. The fact is that we will not know the answer until we actually get there. Until that time comes for us, rather than worrying about being cast into hell if we choose to own a red car, we should be spending the time we have on earth being the best people we can possibly be, to treat each other with more respect and tolerance than is currently being experienced today, because we really should know better by now. Just as Alchemy in the 12$^{th}$ century evolved to become Chemistry, Astrology evolved into Astronomy, Miasma into Germ Theory, and Material Impression became Genetic Theory, then so too should our mere Religionism begin its evolution toward Humanism, at least to start. As we gain more knowledge and tolerance, we should progress still further to a more universal Spiritualism, especially if we suddenly find ourselves not alone in the universe, but in fact part of a broader galactic community comprising of hundreds, if not thousands of unique species and cultures. Unless and until we can stop killing each other over which invisible friend we prefer to believe in, we don't have the slightest hope of leaving our own planet and ensuring the survival of our species. In fact, it wouldn't surprise me if a more militant space-faring species is making plans already to wipe earth's slate clean and nip this savage little group of humanoids in the bud.

So, in an attempt at global enlightenment, the following pages will explore the bible and its assertions, with a 21$^{st}$ century mindset. In essence, to evaluate as many passages as we can in the paper allotted to see if they are still relevant in today's world. To this end, I will focus mainly on the western bible as it stands today, but I will also operate on the presumption that ALL religions, at least in theory, are based on the same fundamental ideologies of peace and tolerance, despite overwhelming historical evidence to the contrary. So sit back, relax, find first gear on the logic centre of your brain, and enjoy the journey!

**HOW TO READ THIS BOOK**

Well, with your eyes, preferably, and starting from the front and working your way to the back. It helps keep track of an already dodgy storyline, it must be said. A skeptical mind open to new possibilities is advantageous, and an imagination rich with inappropriate mental imagery is helpful.

In all seriousness though, it is quite possible that, although you have picked up this book (or even better, actually bought it) with the sole purpose of a chuckle or two, it's equally possible that you haven't gone so far as to have an actual bible in your possession to verify the claims I have asserted. To that end, I have referenced the relevant bible verse/s as and when I cover them, so no additional purchases are required on your part. Of course, you could always take the book with you to the nearest church and either cross-reference it with their bible and/or discuss the discrepancies with your local pastor-priest-cleric-minister-rabbi-pope-whatever. I have personally tested the script at my local church, and it is able to withstand depths of up to 50 paces without smoldering or any other indications of spontaneous combustion, although I probably wouldn't tempt fate by splashing any holy water on it, if I were you. You could also keep a copy next to your front door, strategically feathered with handy Post-It™ sticky-tabs, ready to challenge those wandering God Botherers that interrupt your sleep and always seem to catch you without any rational questions on-hand to confuse them into a rapid retreat. If that's the case, then this book is definitely for you!

Any technical measurements and volumes (such as earth circumference, water volumes, universe size, et cetera) have been calculated as accurately as possible using Mathematics and that most reliable Repository of All Knowledge, Google Search.

It is my sincere hope that, along with a few laughs, you will find your thoughts expanding to consider the incredible yet simple fact of our existence in the universe, and to question any blind obeisance to any organized religions that try to shove themselves down your throat.

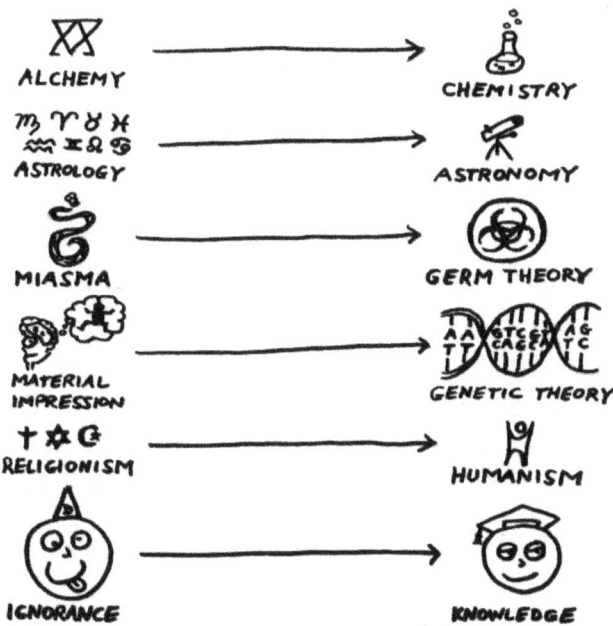

## Genesis 1: In The Beginning

*"In the beginning, there was nothing, which exploded." –Terry Pratchett.*

A lot of Christians nowadays will probably baulk at my starting from Day Dot, preferring the New Testament over the old. But if one is to accurately follow the bible's teachings, they must accept ALL of it, not just the parts they agree with. After all, wasn't it all part of the Divine Plan? We cannot just pick and choose what part of the bible we'll believe and which we choose to ignore because it doesn't suit us, or if it conflicts with other parts of the bible or, in many cases, reality. I don't apologize for dragging these inconvenient discrepancies under the harsh microscope of rational thought, because such beliefs must be based on something slightly more credible than, "because it just is," or "because God said so." I know it's a pretty big ask, but I like my world to be logical and rational. It's just one of my Things™.

So, the Beginning..! Always a great place to start, and what better way to kick things off than to start with literally nothing. No earth, no sun, no stars or planets or galaxies or any of today's modern luxuries. Nothing existed, at all, except this mysterious God guy. And we shall assume male in gender purely for ease of reference; the gender debate aside, I find it hard to think a female could have screwed up the human condition quite as badly as it stands today, assuming there was even a gender to start with. And if we run with this for a moment, how did God consider gender issues at all? If we were created after his own image as the bible often states, should we not all be androgynous, asexual creatures? Remember guys, there was no physical universe: not one reference point - ANYWHERE - to compare any one thing to any other thing. It was nothingness, void, black (we assume, seeing as the lights were still off at this stage), no atoms, no waveforms, no gravity, no time, literally the absence of anything. And this being the case, where was this God guy hanging out prior to him creating all these wonderful flowers and trees and earth and light and heat and yadda yadda yadda? You could argue that he was in heaven, of course, but where, exactly, was that? Even omnipresent beings have to be somewhere, perhaps even another dimension, or a higher plane of existence. Assuming this to be true, how was this place able to exist when there was no universal infrastructure to support it?

Okay, so we have this non-corporeal entity, somehow existing and sentient despite having nothing in the universe by which to support such existence in any way, shape or form, kicking back in his easy-chair sipping his drink, wondering what to do with his next eternity (a neat trick considering the absence even of time).

And he thinks that it would be great if he could create the universe to keep him entertained. A nice big universe, infinitely large, so incredibly massively huge that even to attempt to work out how big it is would leave your brain huddled in the corner crying to itself. The understanding of it so ineffable that it is but a grain of sand in all the atoms of all the observable galaxies in the universe combined, and even then you're just at the infancy of your understanding. And in all that great vast universe, he eventually creates life as we know it on one single solitary ball of rock (we'll get to the flat-Earthers another time).

So great, God thinks this is a fabulous idea, but feels there should be some structure, some meaning to it all. Brimming with immortal confidence, he heads off to his celestial study-come-workshop and draws up a blueprint for the universe – a Divine Plan. It looks good, it looks great; this'll be a cinch! All he needs is, well, everything. Pity the shops are shut at this time of nothing at all. Ah, hell (in the Plan somewhere), he'll just create it all out of nothing. Fabulous piece of wizardry, that, it'll keep 'em wondering how he did it for donkey's years! He's still got all these wonderful things (including donkeys and, for that matter, years) to create, but the juices are flowing now, and he's off to a running start.

Right, first order of business (essentially Day One). God has to have somewhere to put all this neat stuff, so he *"created heaven and earth"* (Gen. 1:1). You have to credit the guy's talent, being able to do all this in the dark, without any physical materials nor any corporeal substance with which to manipulate this matter. Nevertheless, he does this and at this time the earth is *"without form, and void, and darkness was on the face of the deep."* (Gen. 1:2). Well, I should say so, there's no light yet, therefore no means of observation. Additionally, we have the spirit of God *"moving on the face of the waters"*. Now, having personally had several toes severely traumatized over the years by kitchen chair legs, coffee tables and errant Legos or worse, stepping into something cold and slimy the cat hawked up three hours earlier, all lurking in the shadows of the night between you and the bathroom, I can tell you this is no idle achievement. There is also the question of where all this water came from, although by "face of the deep", this may be some obscure passing reference – a tip-of-the-hat, if you will – to the evolutionary process by which we first emerged from the primordial oceans prior to (briefly) swinging about in trees, before growing out of that nonsense and becoming proper bipedal creatures.

So now the big guy gets with the Plan and creates Light. Now I'm no supreme creator by any stretch of the imagination, but if I were, turning on the lights would probably be my first task. It goes a long way toward effectively monitoring your progress. Never mind, better late than never. We have some light on the situation now, and it's good. In a stroke of brilliance, he calls the light "day" and the darkness "night", then contradicts himself royally with the rest of Gen. 1.5: *"And the evening and the morning were the first day."* Not even a single day into his Divine Plan, and he's confused the functions of "light" and "dark", although it could be argued that God was the first shift worker ever to exist.

But I digress. There is no mention of where this light is originating from. There still aren't any stars in the sky (no actual sky, for that matter, but events are progressing rapidly now), no electricity, nothing to generate any sort of EM radiation, visible or otherwise. It's just "there", huddled with the rest of its kind in the corner trying to be brave whilst being surrounded by darkness. Capital.

Okay, so next comes *"the firmament in the midst of the waters, and let it divide the waters from the waters."* (Gen. 1:6 – Gen. 1:8). Furthermore, that this firmament *"divided the waters under the firmament from the waters above the firmament"*. Essentially, an atmosphere, which depending on what version of the book you have is called either "heaven" or "the sky". However the convoluted wording almost makes it sound like heaven is not in the sky, but cleverly tucked away between two bodies of water. No wonder there are so many interpretations to this book!

Okay, now we're on Day three, the middle of the work week, hump day, whatever you choose to call it (Gen. 1.8- Gen. 1:13). This day he creates land, seas (couldn't really help but create them as a consequence of land appearing between the water, so no miracle there), then grass, herbs and fruit trees. Busy lad.

Now my favourite contradiction of them all, Gen. 1:14 – Gen. 1:19. The creation of the sun and moon, and their representation for separating of days, and nights, and years. It really begs the question, doesn't it: If God created the sun on the fourth day, how the hell had four days passed? Until they were created, there was no observable measure of time (not that anyone was alive yet to observe its passage anyway, except this God character) who at this stage seems to be just making it up as he goes along, Divine Plan be damned to hell (another place yet to be created, but the odds are good that its first occupant was the Divine Plan).

Fifth Day: whales, birds, and other manner of creatures to breed and multiply. From my earlier days of playing with plasticine, I willing to bet he made the snakes first, and got creative from there.

Sixth Day: God creates Man, in his own image. And Eve, apparently. Male AND female, both at once (we'll come back to this shortly). And told them to multiply, subdue and tame the earth, and hold dominion over all. Okay, cool.

Seventh Day: God figures he needs a rest, does nothing.

Hmm. Not a very auspicious start to the whole thing, is it? We expect brand new universes to be shaky, violent things, and to break the odd rule occasionally to make things work, within the boundaries of quantum possibility, of course. But for an all-powerful, sentient entity to exist where nothing yet exists is an incredible stretch of credibility, even for the most broadminded of individuals. It's the ultimate expression of, "I think, therefore I am"; the ability to think, and be sentient, without form of any kind (including waveforms) or any medium to support such things. It's like trying to be the words of a storybook without the paper to be words upon. Without the fundamental structure of the universe – the paper – the printed words cannot possibly exist. Even if that story is in the mind of the author, the essence of that story still has a structure in which to exist, that being the spongy lump between said author's ears, cradling the story like a lattice of thought. And therein lies the paradox. Perhaps "God" (for lack of a better term) *is* the universe, beginning existence at one and the same time, and our own lives – who we are, what we learn, what we experience – are merely finger-like protuberances into the material plane, and the knowledge we gather is eventually absorbed into this Universal Consciousness when we shuck our mortal coils? It's something we will never really know, I feel, but for me it does have a certain elegance to the concept, however unable we will ever be to prove one way or the other. However you feel about the theory, it's no more "out there" than some of the stuff we've just covered and we're only one chapter in! If nothing else can be said about our impending odyssey through biblical history, we are at least guaranteed that it will be an interesting one.

## Genesis 2: The Awakening

*"It's exhilarating to be alive in a time of awakening consciousness; it can also be confusing, disorienting and painful."* –Adrienne Rich.

So now we come to the Awakening of man to the newly created world, and we find some fun contradictions here. After having *"completed all the works of heaven and earth in their vast array"* (Gen. 2:1), the Big Guy has a rest. However, Gen. 2:5 through 2:9 clearly states another order: *"No shrub had yet appeared and no plant had sprung up, no rain had yet been sent* (2:5), but God sent forth streams to water the ENTIRE surface of the earth (a pre-flood flood?). THEN God created Man from the dust (2:7), created a garden (Eden, 2:8), followed by all the trees (2:9) clearly making a liar of Gen. 1:13, and once set to work in the garden, creating his animal minions (2:19) to assist Adam in his toils. But animals, generally speaking, aren't that well adapted for tool use, and so God *"caused Adam to fall into a deep sleep"* (Gen. 2:21), during which time, God filched one of Adam's ribs and used it to create Woman.

Okay, a couple of things. The most obvious one being the matter of the nocturnal theft; if God was able to create the entire universe out of, literally, nothing, why did he need Adam's rib to create one more thing?

Now that we have a basic idea of the Dawn of Creation and Man in particular, I'd like to introduce a counterargument to this course of events. Being a lover of logic, technology, the vast universe and the evolution of human morals and ethics, I am naturally drawn to such diversions as Star Trek. Using that as a basis, I would like to hypothesize the following to you, my dear readers:

What if the Garden of Eden was actually a holodeck?

Let's explore this supposition for a while, as logically as we are able with our current knowledge base and a small smattering of guided imagination based on how we need to progress as a species. It may get a bit technical and unwieldy, but I'll try to simplify it wherever possible.

As we already know, the universe is staggeringly, mind-bogglingly huge, with an infinite number of galaxies, stars, and planets. Given the fact that life developed on earth, it's fairly safe to assume that, in some form or another, life has developed elsewhere in the universe as well. In fact, in 1961 Frank Drake constructed the Drake Equation, used to determine the probable number of civilizations in our galaxy (we'll leave the rest of the universe out of it for the time being, however we can assume that any comparably-sized galaxy will generate similar numbers). The original 1961 equation considers the following variables:

$N = R * f_p * n_e * f_l * f_i * f_c * L$

$N$ = the number of civilizations in our galaxy with which communication might be possible;
$R$ = the average rate of star formation in our galaxy;
$f_p$ = the fraction of those stars that have planets;
$n_e$ = the average number of planets that can potentially support life per star that has planets;
$f_l$ = the fraction of planets that could support life that actually develop life at some point;
$f_i$ = the fraction of planets with life that actually go on to develop intelligent life (civilizations);
$f_c$ = the fraction of civilizations that develop a technology that releases detectable signs of their existence into space;
$L$ = the length of time for which such civilizations release detectable signals into space.

Whilst there was heated debate on the values of these parameters, the 'educated guesses' used by Drake and his colleagues in 1961 were:

- $R$ = 1/year (1 star formed per year, on the average over the life of the galaxy; this was regarded as conservative);

- $f_p$ = 0.2-0.5 (one fifth to one half of all stars formed will have planets);

- $n_e$ = 1-5 (stars with planets will have between 1 and 5 planets capable of developing life, i.e. In the Habitable Zone where liquid water can exist on the planet);

- $f_l$ = 1 (100% of these planets will develop life);

- $f_i$ = 1 (100% of which will develop intelligent life);

- $f_c$ = 0.1-0.2 (10-20% of which will be able to communicate);

- $L$ = 1000-100,000,000 years (which will last somewhere between 1000 and 100,000,000 years).

It is interesting to note that, using the lowest numbers available in the equation, the *absolute minimum* number of civilizations in our galaxy alone (N) comes to 20. If we increase the odds to their most favourable, the number of civilizations could easily be 50,000,000. Given the uncertainties as a result of the limited observational technologies of the time, and taking into the account the age of the universe, the original meeting concluded that $N \approx L$, and that there are probably between 1000 and 100,000,000 civilizations in the Milky Way galaxy alone. If we use the lower figure of 1000, it means that there is one intelligent civilization for every 400 million stars. An extremely conservative estimate when you consider that if a thing (e.g. Life) happens, the likelihood of it happening again increases with every subsequent occurrence, given favourable environmental conditions in which to do so.

Today, we know through observations that there are approximately 400 billion stars in the Milky Way galaxy. We have also developed our optical technology to the extent that we have discovered dozens of planets capable of supporting life, seven of which are in the Trappist-1 system alone, a mere stone's-throw at 40 light-years away. Given the propensity of planets in the habitable zone of stars in such close proximity to our own blue-green orb, is it not presumptuous, even downright arrogant, to assume that we are the only form of life in the universe? Especially when you consider that, with our current tech, we have a planet-searching radius of approximately 3000 light-years, or about one tenth of the way to our own galactic central point? I mean, really: God created this massive, stupefying edifice, and we humans are the ONLY ones in it? Seems a bit like keeping your pet ant inside an ant farm the size of, say, Jupiter; there is a massive amount of extra work being done here for negligible benefit. Obviously this otherwise-clever god doesn't know about (or hasn't yet invented) the Law of Diminishing Returns, because a universe of this size with just us to occupy it (and no physical means to reach the rest of it) is an absolute mockery of the concept.

Anyway, back to the holodeck hypothesis, which seems to be an increasingly reasonable hypothesis the more you consider it, and to which I shall no doubt refer throughout this book. Supposing – just supposing – that instead of an invisible man in the sky creating everything we see, this planet was visited by some extra-terrestrial entity? Supposing they stayed for a while, either by choice or by unfortunate circumstance (repairs to their ship, for instance). Now imagine that these beings, with nothing better to do with their time whilst waiting for these repairs or the next ride home, decide to experiment with the indigenous species on the planet. They spot a likely group of ape-like hominids and figure out that they can kick-start their intelligence and other higher brain functions through genetic engineering. Bear in mind at this stage that, if these beings are capable of interstellar flight, genetic resequencing would be a walk in the park for them; indeed, we're dipping our toes into the field even now with genetically modified foods, gene splicing, cloned sheep and other such feats of bioengineering.

Before they start molesting the native fauna, however, these beings need to provide an environment separate from the main group to study the effects of their experiment and to quarantine them should things go awry. Enter, the holodeck. Allow me to run this hypothetical scenario by you, and I'll leave it up to you to determine whether it holds water or not:

The Leader of the Expedition (whom we shall randomly name, "Yaweh") enters the holodeck and turns on the lights (*all is darkness and void, and he said let there be light, and there was light* – Gen. 1.1 – 1:3);

First up, an artificial environment closely resembling that from which Subject A is to be taken (*and he created the waters and the earth and the land and yadda yadda*, Gen. 1:5-1:14). Takes a couple of days to duplicate this with any accuracy;

Then they need to replicate the movement of the sun and moon across the sky of the artificial environment. In conjunction with the rest of the programming, they get the solar and lunar cycles synchronized perfectly after four days (Gen 1:15);

Next is to fill the place with the plants and animals. Lifelike holo-projections are created of the lions, tigers, birds, bats, snakes, et al (Gen. 1:19 – 1:25). Random Side-Thought: Have you ever looked at a pictorial representation of the Garden of Eden, and wondered how Adam and Eve could coexist peacefully with those lions and tigers and other large carnivores? The answer becomes obvious when you entertain the possibility of holograms;

And now, having completed their self-contained habitat, they grab one of the healthier-looking males in the group and inject him with their mental power-up juice. Where there was once an ape-like hominid, you now have a creature on the dawn of intelligence.

Now that Subject A (whom we shall randomly call, "Adam") is capable of thought and learning, the leader introduces Adam to language to better understand the world around him. After a while, Team Leader Yaweh understands Adam's feelings of loneliness and isolation, and resolves to find him a female to keep him entertained. Or at the very least, to keep him from masturbating behind the juniper bushes at every opportunity.

It's at this point that the team discovers that they used almost all of their mental go-go juice on Adam, and there isn't enough serum in production to kickstart a second subject (Project "Eve"). Then one of the team determines that all they need is a bit of bone marrow from Subject A, now creating the modified DNA sequences of their own accord, in conjunction with the rest of the serum, and that should work swimmingly. So Adam *"goes into a deep sleep"* (Gen. 2:21) and wakes up some time later, sans-rib. In today's logical enlightenment, the explanation is simple: anaesthesia and surgery.

Okay, so now our team of intergalactic eggheads have their running experiment, with two genetically modified hominid apes running about a simulated garden-come-laboratory, eating and drinking and learning and fornicating to their heart's content. The team leader is pleased with this, his production of mental serum is recovering, and at this stage decides to see how well their intelligence handles a few simple instructions.

"Go anywhere you want, eat whatever you like," Yaweh says to the pair, "but don't touch anything on that shelf over there."

"Sheh-elf..?" queries Adam.

"Yes, that wooden shelf with the bottles on it," he repeats, pointing to the strangely apple-shaped bottles filled with a reddish liquid. "No touchee, understandee?"

"Okayyy... no touch tree things," Adam replies, eager to please his clever and obviously powerful new master. Satisfied, Team Leader Yaweh leaves them to their devices.

Later on that day, Adam finds Eve raiding the shelves, picking up one of the red apple-shaped bottles.

"Eve! No touchee tree things!"

"Piss on that. Tastes good! You try!"

"Okay..."

And thus, Subjects A and B discovered what it means to be undressed, shortly before Team Leader Yaweh returns from his progress meeting.

"Adam? Eve? What are you doing behind that tree? Wh- OI!!!! WHAT DID I TELL YOU ABOUT TOUCHING THAT SHELF?!! DAFUQ, GUYS!!! I AM SO PISSED OFF WITH YOU

MISERABLE PAIR OF TWATS! KUSHIEL, GET THEM OFF MY BLOODY SHIP, NOW!!!!"

"Right away, sir."

"Goddammit, weeks of faffing around with these half-baked simians when I could've just run the Eroticon 4 holo-program and had some fun. Blah blurgh hmmph etc....."

And so Adam and Eve were unceremoniously booted out of their simulated paradise to suffer and toil the rest of their days.

I can only speak from my own personal standpoint, but based on the events of Genesis alone, I can't help but feel that the Interstellar Explanation is slightly more believable. At least we have most of the physics in place to support the theory, and if you do happen to be an interstellar species, one of the major mission priorities would be to seed your species on as many habitable rocks as you can find. Pretty much exactly what NASA has in mind when exploring such projects as permanent human habitations on Mars, the Moon, or any other base of operation from which the human race could leapfrog into the inky black void of space. The drive to ensure the continuity of one's species is very strong, so it's only logical to conclude that, if we're thinking of space colonization, other species are thinking the exact same thing, and depending on the advance of their technologies relative to our own, we could be quickly outpaced for our nearby resources, or even used as a resource ourselves. It reminds me of a very old PC game I used to enjoy playing called Master of Orion. Brilliant game of expansion, conquest and survival and, starting with one solitary planet and one colony ship, you quickly learned that expansion is the number one goal early in the game. Concentrating on the wrong thing or wasting even one turn was liable to mean the difference between victory and defeat, be it by extermination at the hands of an aggressive species or being outvoted at the galactic council. My point, as always, is that if we don't resolve our differences on this planet, and soon, we may well have lost before we even get started. They say art imitates life (and vice versa), and I can find no more relevant example than this. We are at the dawn of our interstellar lives, the Turn One of our game. Let's not waste it, and our planet's finite resources, with our pathetic, pointless squabbles over who has the goofiest hairstyle or the orangest skin.

## Genesis 3: The Fall, and why talking animals shouldn't be trusted

*"There are rumours circulating that dogs can talk. They're not true. If any dog comes up to you and tells you he can talk, he's lying." - Lame Dog Joke.*

Prior to the infamous Dawn of Bashfulness, we must deal with the Magical Talking Serpent, and Team Leader Yaweh's overreacting, almost schizophrenic temperament. As is related to us in Genesis part three, Eve is "deceived" by the Talking Serpent into partaking of the forbidden goodies, thereby condemning the human race to eternal pain and suffering.

Talking snake? Easy. If we wanted to continue our holodeck explanation, it's not too much effort for a disgruntled team member to fudge with the sound and/or programming to fool Eve into succumbing to temptation. Which, of course she does, and drags Adam along for the ride. But prior to this, and after tasting of the forbidden fruit, Adam and Eve in their nakedness and shame, *"sewed fig leaves together and made clothes for themselves"* (Gen. 3:8). Which begs the question: Even assuming that the fruit of knowledge even contained the concept of sewing and the manufacture of garments, where in that garden (holographic or otherwise) would they have possibly encountered a needle and thread to even attempt the task?

Anyway, for the sin of eating this forbidden fruit, God chucks a massive wobbly and cursed them with a lifetime of pain and suffering and toil and disease and painful childbirths for the rest of their days. In today's age, it sounds almost like the withdrawal of the supply of advanced medicines, able to block pain and prolong life indefinitely. Certainly a spacefaring species would have developed these compounds to counteract the detrimental effects of prolonged interstellar travel, even so far as reversing (or at the very least delaying) the ravages of age.

And now perversely, just as quickly as God's wobbly began, he then personally made garments for Adam and Eve and clothed them both (Gen. 3:21). Doing a bit of good-cop, bad-cop, just to keep 'em guessing. And for a final insult, God says that now his experiments know too much– *"the man has now become like one of us, knowing good and evil"* (Gen: 3:22), he banishes them from all the awesome feel-good eternity drugs and turfs them out on their ears, posting a pair of hardcase midgets at the door (cherubim) armed with flaming swords (light sabres, anyone?) in case they try to sneak back in.

So that's the gripping story of mankind's creation and expulsion from paradise. Great stuff, full of drama and mystery and surprise twists to keep the reader guessing, gaping holes in the plot notwithstanding. One final question for those who still hold onto the belief that the bible version is the literal truth: Who was writing down all this stuff? By this stage of the creation, we have three major players here, being God himself, Adam and Eve. And the Serpent if you want to get picky about it. Maybe a cherubim or two, the creation of whom was so completely glossed over that hardly anyone questions who they are or how (or why, or even when) they were created. So which of these players was recording these events to be spread to a supposed populace of three? God himself? Unlikely, because being an omnipotent being requires that he does not fail at anything, and he's hardly likely to admit fault while he's in his Vengeful God Mode™. Additionally, you would think that being the Supreme Creator of Everything, he could at least be able to afford (or create) a secretary. Adam and Eve? Perhaps, through word of mouth, but who are they going to tell? Do they have enough knowledge of language to preserve those memories onto paper (assuming such exists) and pencil (even more unlikely)? Maybe one of the cherubim wrote it down in his diary after his shift on the east door and moonlighting as a bouncer at the ship's mess hall, and it fell into the wrong hands? The disgruntled team member, perhaps the one who ruined the experiment in the first place by putting words into a holographic snake? I guess we'll never truly know, but it's amusing to explore the possibilities. Throwing a few of these curveballs at your next Sunday callers is bound to have them scrambling for either their bibles or your front gate in a hasty retreat. But don't worry, we haven't even scratched the surface of the things that need questioning. Let us, in the interests of greater understanding and research, continue our expedition!

## Genesis 4: The Population Explosion

So now we come to the juicy bits of the Good Book, full of sex and envy and bloody murder and brutal come-uppances, the hallmarks of any gripping work of fiction. Adam and Eve have been unceremoniously, if confusingly, ejected from paradise with a new set of duds, cut off from their eternity and painkilling drugs, guaranteeing them a shortened life of pain and toil and suffering. Yet despite these overwhelmingly unpleasant sensations, Adam finds he can still get it up, and so introduces Eve to a nasty little surprise called Unmedicated Childbirth. A son called Cain is spawned, followed soon thereafter by another, Abel (Gen. 4:1). Some more time passed, and both sons found something productive to do with their time; one working the land, the other with sheep. Eventually, it came to pass that the sons, probably motivated by their parents' stories of eternal life and the wonderful drugs they enjoyed before they were cast out, decide to curry favour with God with the fruits of their labour; Abel with some nice roast lamb concoction, and Cain with actual fruit. Hmm.

Now God's still quite sore about the whole Applegate thing, but figures there's no harm in accepting the largesse of a free feed. Of course, the hearty lamb roast is the winner of that particular contest (Tom Cruise having not been invented at this stage), and Cain is more than a little pissed about it. He lures his brother out into his field under false pretences, and summarily brains him with a rock. Cain is caught out because he has yet to learn how to dispose of the evidence, whereas God has had at least three millennia to catch up on all the NCIS episodes. He is turfed off his fields and sent to be an aimless wanderer for the rest of his days. Not such a bad thing relatively speaking; the population of the earth was reduced by a whole third (God and his team not included), and there's still 99.9999% of the earth waiting to be discovered and explored, to make a fresh start. Doesn't seem that bad to me.

Instead he pleads to God, saying that he'll be *"hidden from your presence, and anyone who finds me will kill me."* (Gen. 4:14). Er…. who would that be, exactly, out of a population of three? His parents? Sure they're upset about the whole rock thing, but they figure it's probably one of those suffering things God was on about. The rest of the God Squad seem too busy to care about some scuffle between the natives. There are of course the other non-evolved simian primates, but without the benefit of intelligence and a sense of morality, it's hardly likely they'll even care about events beyond their own peer group. It's hard to fathom where he feels this perceived threat is coming from. At any rate, he receives this mysterious identifying mark to let people know not to kill him (persecution complex much?) and off he goes into the wilderness to the east, settling in the Land of Nod, gets jiggy with his wife and fathers a son, Enoch (Gen. 4:16 – 4:18).

A few things scream for clarification here:
- Where did Cain's wife suddenly appear from?
- What was her name?

- Where did this mysterious land, Nod, spring from, and who was living there to give it that name?
- How lucky was Cain to head east to be able to find this suddenly-appearing Nod? Three hundred and sixty unique degrees of direction to choose from, and he hits pay dirt first time.

Furthermore, Cain's son finds a wife and had a son, who did the same, down for five generations. The fifth was lucky enough to find TWO wives (whether separately or concurrently is not divulged). After all this happened, Adam manages to get it up one last time and fathered Seth, claiming that God granted him Seth for the loss of Abel, which leads one to think that the causal relationship between coitus and conception were beyond his limited comprehension, even after all these years. And where all these extra wives have suddenly materialized from remains a mystery to me. Were they prayed for? Do you think that would work if we put all our effort into it? Indications suggest perhaps not. Did God just snap his fingers and will them into existence? Did he dig into his barrel of primordial clay and roll out a couple of wives for them? Perhaps they sprouted out of the ground like mushrooms? It's quite the conundrum, isn't it, if we're to take everything that's been read beforehand as the Truth of Creation. Where *do* you find the extra people necessary to make it all work? I can appreciate that numeracy back then would have been basic at best, but even pre-schoolers frown when you watch them trying to work out the math.

## Genesis 5: Adam researches his Family Tree, finds out he's the Sap.

*"Get your facts first. Then you can distort them as you please." –Mark Twain.*

So now in an attempt to more accurately record all these extra people suddenly floating around in the world without the benefit of either coitus or creation from dust to explain them, the Good Book now starts up a rudimentary family tree. Great idea that, should help with the credibility by putting some solid numbers into the mix. Numbers don't lie, right? Okay then, let's start with Adam, working our way through parts 1 to 31 of Gen 5:

Adam – The first Human – fathered Seth when he was 130 years old. Yes, you read that right. One hundred and thirty years old. And this is Seth we're talking about, not Cain and Abel, but we'll talk about those two later when it's relevant to the argument. So, 130 years old when he fathered Seth, lived a further 800 (eight hundred) years, fathering "other sons and daughters" (names not disclosed), then finally he died at the ripe old age of 930.

Hopefully, this hastily-constructed table will sort out the numbers more clearly:

| Name | Age at 1st Child | Died | Gen. Ref. |
|---|---|---|---|
| Adam | 130 (Seth)* | 930 | 5:5 |

| | | | |
|---|---|---|---|
| Seth | 105 (Enosh) | 912 | 5:8 |
| Enosh | 90 (Kenan) | 905 | 5:11 |
| Kenan | 70 (Mahalalel) | 910 | 5:14 |
| Mahalalel | 65 (Jared) | 895 | 5:17 |
| Jared | 162 (Enoch) | 962 | 5:20 |
| Enoch | 65 (Methuselah) | 365 | 5:24 |
| Methuselah | 187 (Lamech) | 969 | 5:27 |
| Lamech | 182 (Noah) | 777 | 5:31 |
| Noah | 500 (Shem) | 950 | 9:29 |

*(\* Technically the third child, but limited age information exists for the first two.)*

Now, you've probably noticed, with the exception of Enoch, that these buggers seem to be extremely long-lived for humans who are not only at the dawn of civilization, but have also been cursed by God to toil and suffer pain and diseases and all manner of hardships. This is where I'm going to play Devil's Advocate (still no mention of this dude – has he been created yet? I suppose we'll find out in later chapters) and argue for the side of numerical integrity.

Close your eyes, and imagine yourself for a moment as one of these people who are at the dawn of your awareness to your surroundings. You're becoming aware of the passing of time, because you have Day and Night to assist you in this observation. The question I pose to you now is this: How would you determine with any certainty the passing of a longer period of time than a day, and what would you call it? We have, as I say, night and day, great for short-term stuff, but what else? There are no seasons to speak of – remember that, geographyically, you're somewhere in the Middle East, where there is nothing but sand and flies and camel shit forever. Do you have an inkling? Well, I'll put you out of your misery, dear readers: consider, if you will, the moon.

The first men, looking up at the sky at night, would see the moon as a big round silver sun. Then with each passing night, a little bit disappears, until it vanishes completely. Then it reappears in the evening sky, again a sliver of itself, gradually waxing to become full again. One lunar month. These men no doubt observed this wonder, and arbitrarily called it a "year." Let's see how this new information affects the ages of the people in our list:

| **Name** | **Lunar Age** | **(Lunar Age/13)** |
|---|---|---|
| Adam | 930 | 71.5 |
| Seth | 912 | 70.1 |
| Enosh | 905 | 69.6 |
| Kenan | 910 | 70 |
| Mahalalel | 895 | 68.8 |

| | | |
|---|---|---|
| Jared | 962 | 74 |
| Enoch | 365 | 28 |
| Methuselah | 969 | 74.5 |
| Lamech | 777 | 59.7 |
| Noah | 950 | 73 |

Suddenly, those hyper-advanced ages seem a little more believable, don't they? One small additional piece of information, and the numbers become more plausible. Given the benefit of our curiosity and advances in science, we can now ascertain that Noah was actually 38 years old when he fathered his son Shem, and a mere 46 when he built his ark. It would certainly have been easier to manhandle those elephants when he was 46 than when he was 600, that's for sure! More on that later.

# Genesis 6: Back to the Drawing Board.

*"Mistakes were made. Others were blamed." Darynda Jones.*

The human population has found its niche and is growing exponentially, like any good plague, especially with the assistance of wives appearing, literally, out of thin air to marry all these descendants of Adam. We are now introduced to the inevitable consequence of gods and men living together, which is interspecies procreation. Humans are breeding sons AND daughters of course, as any species will, and the big guy is suddenly finding that the "Sons of God" are marrying and pro-creating with the "daughters of men" (Gen. 6:1 – 6:2).

Who are these "Sons of God", and where did *they* grow from? Is it a reference to Adam's descendants, who have started marrying all these daughters of... whom? Where did all these extra people come from, if it's only Adam's descendants on the planet (assuming, for the sake of decency, that incestuous goings-on has already been tabooed somewhere; I certainly haven't seen it as yet)? And if incest is the case here, the genetic complications assoc-iated with in-breeding certainly would NOT result in "beautiful daughters", unless a cleft palate and mental retardation floats your boat.

The second explanation is that the Sons of God were "angels", ethereal spirit entities (like God) who are getting jiggy with the daughters of men. Essentially, incorporeal entities who are impregnating women without any physical means of procreation (i.e. physical bodies, DNA transfer, et al). A precursor to the immaculate conception, as such. But we're still left in the dark about where they came from. Whichever explanation you prefer, it seems obvious that God has been burning the midnight oil either making new people out of the dust or more gods, which would seriously impact on his omnipotence, if he had other gods running about wreaking havoc with unsanctioned miracles and such.

A more likely explanation goes back to our interstellar visitor scenario, where the ship's crew, having been stranded in this poxy little backwater for the last hundred years or so (1,556 "bible years" divided by 13 months, give or take a year or 20) are getting tired of the same old holo-porn and yearn for some actual sex with a living thing instead of, essentially, computerised masturbation. So when all these "daughters of men" start maturing and developing their interesting bits, what red-blooded *(major* assumption) humanoid alien would be able to resist a bit of how's-your-father? "Hey, babe, how about you and me come back to my ship for some fun? I'm almost god-like, you know; done some miracles of my own in my day... damn, but you look *fine*, girl!!" I can see it all now, those polyester-leisure-suit-wearing interstellar bastards...

Whatever the explanation, God is now getting sick of this intrusion of humans into his daily life, hanging around for years and years, messing up the joint and generally getting underfoot, and decides to impose some limits. He decides in his infinite wisdom (or more likely, he'd just finished watching *Logan's Run* the night before) that the human life span *"will be one hundred and twenty years" (Gen 6:3)*.

A hundred and twenty years, huh? Okay then, assuming we're still working on "bible-years", that means that the new lifespan of humans will be roughly *nine years and two months*. Seems a bit harsh to me; at least the people in *Logan's Run* were allowed to live until they were thirty. And if God was referring to solar years as they perceived them through their advanced knowledge, then this would actually ADD another fifty years (on average) to the human lifespan, which exacerbates the problem rather than solving it. Although, if this restriction was indeed effected (through divine will, imperial degree, or ratification by committee), it might go a long way toward explaining the predilection for certain religions to marry and breed with six-year-old girls (assuming no camels were readily available, that is).

And now we have a name for the inter-species offspring of "angels" and humans: Nephilim (Gen. 6:4). According to legend, and interpretations made by historians from such texts as the Dead Sea Scrolls and other Hebrew writings, these Nephilim were the medieval equivalent of giants. Huge humanoid creatures of immense strength and size, "heroes of old, men of renown". Well, I suppose if you're hulking about the place with your 20 feet of height and size 93 sandals, it's going to be pretty easy to pull off heroic feats like bench-pressing oxen or pile-driving your enemies. Normal men would see how handy these guys would be in a fight, and probably contrived to get them involved in their own selfish affairs, providing the muscle needed to get that birth-right back and so on.

God, however wasn't impressed by this development, and decided at this stage to just scrap the whole lot and start again (Gen. 6:6 – 6:7). But wait a minute..! Wasn't all this in the Divine Plan? Why would God get all upset and angry over something that he planned to happen in the first place? This was the game plan, wasn't it? And now the plan isn't working the way he likes (even though he was supposed to have seen all this happening ahead of time), he wants to hit the Reset Button on it all and start from scratch? Something's not right here. It's not much of a Divine Plan if any idiot can alter it with a simple act of Free Will. But not all is lost, because our old mate Noah has been in God's good books for a while now (a nice guy, keeps to himself, has an unhealthy obsession with animals, though), and it is he that God now recruits to help sort this mess out.

And this, too, gives me cause for concern. This omnipotent being, replete with mystical, terrifying powers, needs the help of a mere human to reboot the system? Why doesn't he just snap his ethereal fingers, nod his head, wiggle the nose, press the big red RESET button, and have the whole mess vanish in a puff of nothingness? It certainly seems to be a very simple solution, for a god. After all, mothers all over the world have at some stage threatened their kids, "I brought you into this world, I can take you out of it...!" God supposedly created everything out of literally nothing (notwithstanding needing that one rib earlier in the peace), so why can't he now just UNcreate it? Go back, revise the plan in his little floaty-space of nothingness, tweak the parameters, iron out the bugs, and start again bright and early Monday morning? Hell, since we're redoing the whole shebang anyway, let's make it Rumday morning. Mondays sucked, anyway...

So as a result of some seriously righteous sycophancy (*"Noah was a righteous man, blameless among the people of his time, and he walked faithfully with God"*, Gen. 6:9), Noah kicks back with God and discusses the end of the world as they know it (Gen 6:10- 6:13). It would seem that, even though he's still pissed about the whole Applegate saga and booted humanity out on its disobedient arse, he's still wandering around on the planet, checking things out, observing all the evil and wickedness and Him-knows-what going on in this, his greatest creation, with Noah nipping at his heels like an eager puppy. It seems strange that God would choose to observe events this way instead of, say, in his ethereal, omnipresent capacity; but then who am I to argue over semantics? There are that many people on the earth by this stage, both mundanely born of men and others magically appearing out of thin air, that trying to watch them all at once would probably cause a stroke. And because Noah is just a normal man, I'm going to go with the option that God was walking with him, rather than Noah being zapped off to heaven to kick it with God over some brewskis because, as far as I'm aware, nobody has returned from heaven just yet. Not alive, at any rate.

Anyway, back to the story. God's pissed with how this Earth thing is going with its violence and selfishness and general debauchery and wants to wash his hands of the lot of it. And it occurs to God that he could bloody well do just that: drown the whole sodding lot and screw 'em if they can't take a joke. But even in his pissed-off state, he has a soft spot for old Noah, even if he does come off a little sycophantic. So he tells Noah to build a big-arse boat to carry his family and his pet collection so that when the flood comes they'll survive (Gen. 6:12 - 6:13). Again, it would be so easy to snap his fingers and dice the lot - even keeping the bits he wanted wouldn't be too much effort for an omnipotent being - but instead he chooses to screw with his recently-created minions, I suppose if only to relieve the boredom, and see how many hoops they're prepared to jump through.

And I suppose when you think about that for a moment, isn't that what it's really all about, assuming these things really did occur? If there was an immortal, eternal Creator, who created everything out of nothing, what would it mean to that creator to realize that he's faced with that eternity himself? Until he created the universe, there was nothing, not even time; there WAS no such concept. But when the universe was created - when the heavens and stars and planets and everything else was brought into existence and set in motion, time was the by-product; otherwise, everything would happen at the same time as everything else. So for an immortal being, the prospect of watching all this mind-numbing existence roll out every moment of every day, and being awake for every interminable second of it, would be enough to unbalance anyone, even a god. And we're only a hundred years or so into the experiment so far; we have untold millennia ahead of us! We can almost imagine one of God's eyelids twitching in our mind's eye as his cheese starts to slide off his proverbial cracker. No wonder he thought it'd be a laugh to see Noah madly scrambling to build a big-arse boat in the middle of the desert.

But enough on God's developing instability for now. Suffice to say that he instructs Noah to build this boat, made of cypress wood (I'm not even going there with finding wood in the middle of the desert, so let's assume for the sake of argument that he managed to source the wood somehow, either through purchase, barter or hacking a nearby forest to death). God then outlines the dimensions: 300 cubits long, 50 cubits wide, and 30 cubits high, with a roof on top that leaves a one cubit gap between the roof and the ark, and three decks, imaginatively named lower, middle and upper. Shouldn't take too long for a 600 year old man (46.13 proper years) to knock all that together, right?

But then, what is a cubit, exactly? Officially, it is the measurement of your forearm, from your elbow to the tip of your fingers, and is generally accepted to be approximately 45.72cm. That is, however, a little too simplistic. The Hebrew's short cubit was 44.5cm, while the Egyptian cubit measured 44.7cm. Later on, the Babylonians considered a cubit to be 50.3cm, and the Hebrews and Egyptians also had "long cubits" (essentially, an armlength plus a handwidth) measuring 51.8cm and 52.3cm respectively. Even more confusing is the fact that when the ark was supposedly being built, there was only one measurement of cubit, which historians are yet to agree on without resorting to bloodshed. So considering the variables at the time of construction – the availability of cypress forests in desert regions, the eagerness of Noah to please his god and the rapidly approaching deadline of a flood to kill everything on earth – Noah might have used a standard cubit (45.72cm). Given this measure, the ark would have been 137.6m long, 22.86m wide and 13.7m high over three decks, which when you factor in wood thickness of the deck to support the weight of thousands of animals and the thickness of the hull itself, works out to about 4 metres high per deck. Considering that the height of your average female giraffe is about 4.6 metres and the males average somewhere between five and six metres, it may explain the large lumps they have on their heads. I hope

Noah had the sense to put them on the upper deck...

Noah was then told to chuck his family inside this wooden monstrosity, along with *"two of every animal, male and female, two of every bird, two of pretty much everything that crawled the earth, along with every kind of food to keep them and these animals alive during this flood"* (Gen. 6:19-6:21). No one quite knows how this was managed, but old Noah Doolittle managed it.

## Genesis 7: Time to get wet.

*"Often it does seem such a pity that Noah and his party didn't miss the boat. –Mark Twain.*

So now God has finally got a handle on this flood business and how he's going to achieve it, and tells Noah to grab his family and put them on the ark. He then tells Noah to "*take with you seven pairs of every kind of clean animal, a male and its mate, and one pair of every kind of unclean animal, a male and its mate, also seven pairs of every kind of bird, male and female, to keep their various kinds alive throughout the earth.*" (Gen. 7:2 – 7:3).

Wait…what..??! Anyone who's ever had to endure a biblical flood sermon has had it beaten into them that there were TWO of every animal on the ark, not SIXTEEN (seven clean pairs, one unclean pair). And yet it's right there, in black and white in the bible. Eight pairs, not one. The discrepancy is as inexplicable as it is dumbfounding. If the bible is to be accepted as a true record of events, then God has now clearly snapped under the strain, his remaining sanity huddled in a distressed ball in the corner babbling incoherently to itself while his super-Ego is yelling at trees to stop being so Tuesday; to say nothing of the sheer panic Noah gets when he suddenly has to find seven more breeding pairs of each animal at the eleventh hour (not to mention additional foodstuffs).

While we're speaking of arks and animals, I'd like to step back for a moment and talk about the logistics of this grand adventure. Noah will soon have an ark of wood, stuffed to the rafters with sixteen of every kind of animal (7 clean pairs, one unclean pair) plus his family. He also has stored in this ark enough foodstuffs to feed everyone and everything on this ark for an as-yet undetermined length of time (the bible cites 150 days afloat, just shy of four months). For the sake of argument, we'll assume that supplying water to the animals isn't going to be an issue, if you ignore the rotting corpses of all the earth's unluckier creatures contaminating the water.

Now, the average African elephant will need to consume approximately 250kg of plant matter per day to remain healthy. So to keep just one elephant on a boat for 150 days would require you store approximately 37,500kg of plant matter. Two elephants would make that 75 tonnes, and if Noah managed to rustle up 7 more mating pairs at short notice, he would also have to procure the food for them, which would then weigh 600 tonnes. And that's just the African elephants, ignoring the Indian elephants, or the nearly 350 different species of elephants thought to have existed in the world at one time. Giraffes require about 30kg of food per day, or 4,500kg for the cruise for one giraffe, or 72 tonnes for eight pairs. A cow will get by on about 12kg of hay every day, for a total of 28,800kg to keep sixteen head of cattle healthy. A white rhinoceros will eat about 65kg of food per day, so there's another 156 tonnes of plant matter. So far we have covered only four different species of animal, and their food stores are already well over 800 tonnes. We haven't covered goats, camels, lions, tigers, sheep, ocelots, pangolins, jaguars, pumas, dogs, cats, ostriches, zebras, emus, rabbits, horses, oxen, hyenas.... the list goes on.

And all of this takes space. Even if you allot an entire deck to the storage of foodstuffs (let's hope it wasn't the lower deck, because shit, as always, flows downhill), this leaves two decks for the animals and humans, which works out at approximately 6,270 square meters of floor space. A single elephant will require about 37.16 square metres of space to humanely house the animal, so sixteen will require just under 594 square metres, or roughly 9.48% of the available floor space in the ark. Rhinoceroses (rhinoceri?) would require similar needs, along with other animals on the beefier side. And we haven't begun to consider methods of preventing food spoilage, the birth of animals during their stay, the segregation of carnivores from other animals, the natural demise of undoubtedly a few, or the removal of animal solid and liquid waste (the logical assumption is that it was all tossed overboard, improving the quality of the water supply not one iota). Unless of course, they stored the waste in the space previously occupied by the foodstuffs to preserve the weight of ballast, but you wouldn't want to have them too close together if you could at all help it. A moot point if the lower decks were used for storage, due to animal urine soaking through to the decks below and pooling.

The smell would have been incredible.

Now that we've had a small dose of reality, we shall plunge back into the written account of this biblical flood. God has given Noah a week to find all these extra animals (and food for them); Noah's then shoehorned them into his boat, and after seven days the flood waters came onto the earth. Now comes the really interesting part of this saga, in Gen. 7:11:"*In the six hundredth year of Noah's life, on the seventeenth day of the second month – on that day all the springs of the great deep burst forth, and the floodgates of the heavens were opened.*"

All of a sudden, we have months as a unit of time measurement. Where did this great insight of timekeeping come from? The only reasonable explanation to this conundrum is that God revealed the true nature of the earth's orbit around the sun to Noah; but if this is the case, why is Noah still claiming to be six hundred years old? We cannot reconcile the existence of months without radically recalibrating Noah's age to account for them. Perhaps the author of the bible – either one of Noah's family or God himself, because everyone else was too busy drowning to write anything down – was too mentally feeble to realise the paradox, or hadn't yet learned long division. Whatever the reason, it would have to be a very good one for me to believe that this tale has any basis in truth.

No matter, we shall press on. Noah stuffed all these wild and domestic creatures great and small into the ark, followed by his family and himself when the rains finally came and the land began to flood. *"The animals going in were male and female of every living thing, as God had commanded Noah. Then the Lord shut him in."* (Gen. 7:16). So God, standing outside in the rain, shut the door on the ark. Now I'm not particularly worried about God's safety at this point, with his apparent immortality and whatnot, but it does beg the question of why he wasn't watching these proceedings from on high, shutting the ark door with a wave of his omnipotent hand instead of mucking about in the mud wrestling with a primitive locking mechanism while panicked, screaming people were mobbing the boat trying to get in.

It all seems very implausible doesn't it, readers? Trillions of gigalitres of water suddenly erupting from the ground and the heavens, drowning the entire earth except for one animal-filled boat. And yet there is a theory which proposes that just such a thing could possibly have happened, a theory proposed by Dr. Walt Brown called The Hydroplate Theory (consult that wonderful repository of the modern age, Conservapedia.com, for more details). In its most basic form, it suggests that earth's original Pangea was atop a vast sub-crustal ocean, sealed beneath the crust which was supported by a number of pillars, some fifty miles beneath the surface of early earth's Pangea.

In the Fall of Man as described, these pillars collapsed (or were deliberately destroyed) and the crust created such pressure on the sub-crustal ocean that it was violently expelled from the ground, causing colossal flooding equaling the account in the bible. The Pangea broke apart from this wholesale collapse and created the continents we see today (or remarkably like them). Indeed, the world's landmasses could be arguably compared to a massive jigsaw puzzle, the shattered remnants of the original Pangea. The question we need to ask ourselves most objectively is this: Was the collapse of the pillars of Pangea one of natural erosion, or were extra-terrestrial activities responsible for the collapse?

Let's consider our Spaceman Scenario: Team Leader Yaweh, knowing far more about the composition of the planet due to his advanced technology, and having created a race of hybrid aliens from the primitive ape-like hominids, suddenly finds his creation getting completely out of hand. Knowing that this hybrid experiment will eventually overwhelm the planet, and recognizing they will eventually challenge the omnipotence of the extra-terrestrial visitors (especially as they're already interbreeding with his peeps), Yaweh figures the most effective way to wipe out this experiment is to destroy key pillars supporting the Pangea, causing planet-wide flooding, massive tsunamis, with enough water expelled at extreme pressure into the atmosphere to make it, indeed, rain for forty days and nights and cover the earth with water, or to make it so appear as the shattered Pangea sinks beneath the waves. However, not wanting to completely destroy the planet and its innocent fauna, he contrives with whom Yaweh considers the least corrupt of his experiments (Noah) and orders the ark built for these animals.

It sounds fantastical, but there is evidence that part of this subcrustal ocean survived the cataclysm; a large body of subterranean water under Asia called the Beijing Anomaly, which is roughly the size of the Arctic Ocean in volume, with no explanation of why it might be there. Animal fossils have been found at the highest altitudes, which could well occur in such a catastrophic tectonic upheaval. But while creationists might be jumping up and down at this point screaming that this constitutes proof that the Great Flood occurred, it does not automatically prove the existence of God. It proves, at best, that a cataclysmic event occurred in the dawn of mankind, and that mankind colluded with a physical being of superior knowledge and technology to correct an error of judgment. Nothing more.

For more information concerning the Hydroplate Theory and the hypothetical real-world repercussions to mankind, do yourself a favour and punch "Hydroplate Theory" into your nearest Google search. It is a fascinating theory for the curious sceptic to sink their teeth into, but it is diverting from our narrative through the chapters of Genesis, so I will place it under, "Recommended Reading" and leave it to its own devices for now.

### Genesis 8: You had ONE job, Noah..!

*"Religion is induced insanity." –Madalyn Murray O'Hair.*

So the end of Genesis 7 saw our intrepid hero, Noah, huddled up inside a big-arsed wooden boat surrounded by his wife, his sons and other family, countless thousand animal species and foodstuffs to feed them, and a stench that would gag a rat. Now the rains have stopped, and the S.S. Gopherwood is adrift on an endless sea with no visible means of propulsion (not that there's anywhere to go, mind you, but you'd think there would have been at least a fleeting thought during construction about some rudimentary propulsion, or even station-keeping abilities). After all, the currents generated from flood waters and rainfall sluicing down from hills and over mountains would carry the ark pretty much anywhere else on the planet except the place it originated, especially after nearly four months afloat (again, assuming the combined weight of animals and cargo permitted buoyancy in the first place).

Now God, *"remembered Noah and all the wild animals and the livestock that were with him in the ark, and he sent a wind over the earth, and the waters receded"* (Gen. 8:1). After one hundred and fifty days of floating about like a cork, God suddenly remembered the only living people left on the face of the planet. What was God doing all this time, to make him forget that the world's entire population was stuffed into a boat surrounded by wild animals, many of them carnivorous? I mean sure, you could argue that these animals were rendered docile by the Will of God; but like any exercise in concentration, once you begin to lose focus, the effects tend to wear off fairly quickly. A four month lapse of concentration would not result in a favourable outcome, even in the most optimistic of circumstances. It's not as if God had a lot of other things on his plate at the time, having just drowned a significant portion of them. Perhaps this answers a concern of mine, in that I was never able to figure out how they saved two of every fish while drowning the rest of them. Perhaps, God was otherwise occupied huddling two (sixteen) of every fish and their food into a clean, habitable bubble of a completely inadequate size for the task. One more mystery solved, huzzah!

The waters eventually receded, and *"on the seventeenth day of the seventh month, the ark came to rest on the mountains of Ararat."* (Gen. 9:4). The waters then *"continued to recede until the tenth month, and on the first day of the tenth month the tops of the mountains became visible"* (Gen. 9:5). So by this stage the ark has been adrift for five months, and three months after that they were still unable to leave the ark. This is more than double our original time estimates, and we're not even close to finished with this flood yet. So unless Noah either doubled the amount of foodstuffs or was starving the animals, mealtimes were going to start getting more competitive. So Noah sent a raven out to scout the earth for, well, earth, to no avail. Then over the next three weeks he sent out a dove.

The first time *"the dove could find nowhere to perch because there was water all over the surface of the earth; so it returned to Noah on the ark"* (Gen. 8:9). But the ark had already settled on the earth (Mount Ararat) three months previously, indicating the contrary to be true. But let's ignore that for a moment and consider the dove for a moment. One day a week for three weeks, this dove has been sent to scour the face of the earth for land, an area of some 510 million square kilometres. Considering that a dove flies on average about 30-40 metres from the ground, that gives the dove a maximum sighting distance of 45.2km, horizon-to-horizon. With a circumference of 40,675km (not allowing for the increased circumference due to all that damn water), reducing to about 21,000km towards the north and south poles, we can average that out to about 30,000km in circumference, allowing for small circumnavigations at the poles, and longer trips around the equatorial region.

So with these figures in mind, our biblical dove would have to circumnavigate the planet 663 times. Given a maximum flight speed of 88km/h, the dove would complete its mission, at its absolute earliest:

30,000km average per circumnavigation times 663 circumnavigations = 19,890,000 straight-line km;

Divide by maximum flight speed of 88km/h = 226,022.72 hours flight time required;

Divide by 24 hours = 9417.61 days flight time;

Divide by 365.25 = 25.78 years.

That's 25.78 years of flying at maximum speed, without food or rest, to scour the complete surface of the planet for signs of land. That poor little bastard. And when you consider the average lifespan of a dove is between seven and eleven years, this becomes even more improbable. The longest recorded lifespan of a dove is 31 years if it's looked after, so it's unlikely that it would have made even one trip, let alone three.

Of course, if Noah was more practically-minded, he might have chosen a bird renowned for speed, perhaps a Peregrine falcon. With a cruise altitude of one kilometre (giving the bird a sighting distance of about 224km horizon-to-horizon) and a maximum flight speed of 390km/h, the falcon (also without food or rest) could complete the task in a mere 133 circumnavigations, taking just over a year:

30000km * 133 circumnavigations = 3,990,000 straight-line kilometres;

Divide by 390km/h = 10,230.76 hours flight time required;

Divide by 24 hours = 426 days

Divide by 365.25 = 1.16 years.

Talk about your flights of fancy. To complete its mission in the overly optimistic 12 hours allotted by Noah (i.e. sent out in the morning, returning by the evening), the dove would need to have achieved a flight speed (assuming average height of 40m for a dove) of 1,657,500km/h. Put into perspective, this is about 460km per second, just slightly faster than the speed of the solar wind streaming from our sun, or roughly 1,342 times the speed of sound.

More realistically, we can safely assume that the dove isn't really searching the *entire* earth, but rather the immediate area surrounding the ark (at best, about 23,865 square kilometres, 22.6km visibility horizon-to-horizon at 40m flight height, at 88km/h for 12 hours, assuming a lazy circle around the ark and not overlapping any part of the search area). A bit short of the 510 million square kilometres expected of it, but it is only a dove, after all. But because the bible specifically mentioned the *entire* surface of the earth (Gen. 8:9), it was necessary to illustrate the physical impossibility of the task with the biblically-supplied variables.

So anyway, Noah sent this same bird out a couple more times, firstly returning with an olive branch (apparently, trees were not adversely affected by being submerged in water for eight months), and the next time did not return at all, leaving Noah with one dove to repopulate the species. I hope he sent the male out, and that the female was already impregnated by this stage. And on the subject of trees, it's interesting to note their survival when you consider that photosynthesis is no longer possible in water depths below 200 meters, and no sunlight at all can penetrate below 1000m. Even assuming Mt. Ararat was the tallest mountain known to man at this stage, its height is 5,137 metres above sea level. Ararat also has an ice peak extending down to 3,900 metres above sea level. This would mean that any olive trees must be below the snow line, as olive trees prefer dry, warmer environments such as the Mediterranean to flourish. Now if the ark had indeed settled on Mt. Ararat and Noah sent the dove off to look for land, the highest possible olive tree would have been at least 1,237m beneath the waves, in a pitch-black watery tomb for the past eight months. How healthy can we expect this (or any) olive tree to be under these conditions? My guess would be, "not very." More than likely, the little bugger snuck back into the Ark while Noah wasn't looking and snaffled a branch from the food stores, but then after eight months in storage it wouldn't exactly be fresh, would it?

So now we are told that *"by the first day of the first month of Noah's six hundred and first year, the water had dried up from the earth"* (Gen. 8:13), and that *"by the twenty-seventh day of the second month, the earth was completely dry"* (Gen. 8:14). Now considering that Noah and his menagerie boarded the ark on the second month of his six hundredth year, they have now been bottled up in the thing for one year and ten days. I would imagine that the animals would be chewing on the hull by this stage and keeping a very wary eye on the carnivores.

So now God reappears and *"says to Noah, 'come out of the ark, you and your wife and your sons and their wives'" (Gen. 8.15)*. And thus Noah opened the ark, despite having been locked in it from the outside by God himself (Noah must have had long arms, or used a stick) and led his tribe from the boat, followed by all the animals and birds and all the crawling things. The ordeal is over, the animals have been saved, and the earth is pure from wickedness again, huzzah!

Then *"Noah built an altar to the lord and, taking some of all the clean animals and clean birds, he sacrificed burnt offerings on it"* (Gen. 8.20).

I literally can't even. You had one job, Noah. ONE job: Save the animals. And now that has been achieved against impossible odds, your very first act after saving the animals is to erect an altar and start killing them with fire. What the actual FUCK, man?!?!!? Working our way through a little case of cabin fever, are we? Or more likely, you've picked up a nasty case of Cryptococcal meningitis from one year's cumulative exposure to bird droppings and it's turned your brain into tofu. But the really amazing thing is that God is okay with this (*"The lord smelled the pleasing aroma and said in his heart, 'Never again will I curse the ground because of humans, even though every inclination of the human heart is evil from childhood"* (Gen. 8:21))! But hey, we've already established in Genesis 6 that God's elevator doesn't quite reach the penthouse, so I suppose this, at least, shouldn't be a great surprise to us. Further: *"As long as the earth endures, seedtime and harvest, cold and heat, summer and winter, day and night, will never cease"* (Gen. 8:22). So now we have seasons. Not all of them, just the two major ones, materializing out of nowhere. Perhaps the massive increase in water volume and the currents created (which didn't affect the global positioning of the ark beyond plonking it on top of Mt. Ararat) were enough to tilt the axis of the earth by the 23.5 degrees necessary to create discernible seasons. That's if you can reconcile in your mind the appearance (and subsequent disappearance) of 2.6 trillion gigalitres of water (2,619,870,000,000,000,000,000 litres), which would only just cover the top of Mt. Ararat, let alone any additional water to obscure it in the watery depths. If we want to be pedantic and cover the top of Mount Everest as well (8,848m above sea level) – and surely we'd have to, if we were to adhere to the covering of the *entire* earth with water – you would have to find, and eventually dispose of, at least 4.51 trillion gigalitres of it (4,512,480,000,000,000,000,000 litres). And even if we can process this mind-bubbling number with any success, we still haven't considered the ambient temperature drop and thinning of the atmosphere resulting from being redistributed across the greater surface area of the earth, increasing from 510 million square kilometres to a robust 2.9 billion square kilometres.

Given these insane volumes, I feel that we should err on the side of caution and entertain the possibility that the bible isn't exactly the gospel truth some claim it to be.

## Genesis 9: God admits he went a little O.T.T. with the whole Flood Thing

*"Mistakes are the usual bridge between inexperience and wisdom." –Phyllis Theroux.*

So God's now managed to get a grip, had some Alone Time™, and got things back to a more manageable level. The world's wicked population has been drowned and washed away without so much as a decomposed, fish-eaten corpse to be seen anywhere, the trees have survived their year under the waves without a single mote of light to even illuminate them, let alone sustain them, and everything is as if the flood never happened. And as a bonus prize for Noah, God now commands him to go forth and be fruitful. Additionally, *"the fear and dread of you will fall upon all the beasts of the earth, and all the birds in the sky, on every creature that moves along the ground, and on all the fish in the sea"* (Gen. 9:2). Additionally, *"everything that lives and moves about will be food for you. Just as I gave you the green plants, I now give you everything"* (Gen. 9:3). Awfully decent of the god to give Noah carte blanche to stuff whatever he likes into his gob, but then gives the animals a fear of him so as not to make it too easy to grab a bite to eat. My personal theory is that, after a year being cooped up in a wooden box and starved for a good deal of that time, the animals and birds were more than eager to put as much distance between them and the ark-prison as possible. In fact, had Noah approached any of those animals in the following days, they were more apt to think he was going to stuff them back into the hated wooden box, and screw THAT for a joke. The only real winners of the whole deal were probably the termites, who would've made short work of whatever they hadn't eaten of the ark during their voyage.

God makes a couple of caveats to this, however, and forbids the eating of meat *"that has its lifeblood still in it"* (Gen. 9:4), and that for his lifeblood God *"will surely demand an accounting"* (Gen. 9:5), not just for every animal, but from every human for the life of another human. In essence, God is indicating that he's washing his hands of the lot of 'em, and handing over the punishment of evil acts to their respective peer groups. I'm not sure exactly how this is going to work, because there's no real point of imposing rules and sanctions on people if you're not going to enforce them, essentially handing over that enforcement to the people to whom these sanctions apply.

So now God establishes his famous covenant with Noah and the survivors of the great flood, throwing up a pretty rainbow in the sky as a sign of this covenant, a clever trick considering there had been no rainfall since the 40-day deluge. Anyway, this rainbow signifies God's promise (pinky-swear!) that he will never again destroy all life by the waters of a flood. Undoubtedly great relief for those survivors, having just emerged from a claustrophobic gopherwood purgatory, until you realise that God still has a few elements to play with, such as earth, wind and fire. A vengeful god can get pretty creative with those if he had a mind to, as well as the more exotic methods of plague and disease (which we shall see soon enough). But for now, we have an ironclad pinky-swear that God won't get all vengeful and drown our sorry arses in another flood, and we're grateful that we've got even that assurance from him, and most of the survivors for their part resolve not to push his buttons again anytime soon.

## The Sons of Noah: The Unfairness of Drunken Bastards

We are now told that Noah had three sons, named Shem, Ham and Japheth, and that Ham has a son called Canaan (Gen. 9:18). It is said that *"from these three sons came the people who were scattered across the whole earth"* (Gen. 9:19). In the meantime, Noah had established a nice little vineyard, being a man of the soil and probably still dealing with the Cryptococcus infection running amok in his increasingly-scrambled synapses. So after he drank his first batch of wine, he became wonderfully drunk and ended up in a stupor inside his tent, naked as the day he was born (Gen. 9:21). Now Ham (father of Canaan) saw his father naked and raced outside and told his two brothers of his discovery. The brothers Shem and Japheth contrived to drape a garment between them, and then entered Noah's tent (*backwards, so as not to see their father's naked body*) and draped the garment over him (Gen. 9:23).

Now this is why some people shouldn't drink. When Noah awoke from his stupor and *"found out what his youngest son had done to him"* (Gen. 9:24), he said, *"Cursed be Canaan!! The lowest of slaves he will be to his brothers!"* He also heaps praise on Shem, extends Japheth's territories, permits Japheth to use Shem's tents, and assigns Canaan to be slave to all of them. (Gen. 9:25 – 9:27).

What an arsehole! What did Canaan do to deserve that? It was his sodding father, Ham, who raced out to tell his brothers, and probably only to alert them to the situation rather than any attempt to embarrass his boozy father. But instead of dealing with Ham and discerning his motives, he takes it out on the grandson. Yeah, well played, you crazy old wino. This behaviour carried on for another 350 years (26.92 years; they've somehow lost the knowledge of the new timekeeping, and have reverted to the old system), whereon he finally died at the age of 950 (73, Gen. 9:28 - 9:29). I'm guessing it was neck-and-neck whether it was the liver cirrhosis or the Cryptococcus meningitis that did for him, but without forensic examination we can only speculate.

## Genesis 10: The Splitting of the Three

And so it eventually came to pass that, after the Unpleasantness of the Naked Drunky Father, Shem, Japheth and Ham went their separate ways and populated the earth, creating three separate nations: The Japhethites, the Hamites, and the Semites (why it wasn't Shemites following the method of his brothers is anyone's guess. Some people just need to be individuals). There follows a comprehensive list of the clans within each of the tri-nations, each apparently with their own territories and language, which I won't go into here for the simple reason that it's so damned boring. If you're so inclined, feel free to consult your nearest bible to get up to speed, but it's not strictly necessary to know, other than the fact it's there. It's okay, go on if you must; I'll wait right here, fingers paused quivering over my keyboard, until you get back. If you want to put the kettle on while you're there, I take my coffee white with two sugars, thanks..

So, from Noah's three sons, we are suddenly faced with a total of seventy five separate clans, each with their own language. From one language, we now have over six dozen separate nations now incapable of talking to each other because they've suddenly developed different, separate, complete dialects. Was this to prevent clan secrets from being shared between other clans, whilst still retaining a universal common tongue? Or was it simple local variations evolving over time and distance to become a unique language in its own right? Whatever the cause, the peoples of the earth are now becoming divided and mistrustful of each other due to the breakdown of universal understanding through a common tongue.

Although a small chapter, it's nonetheless important to mention all these different languages being developed, because of the next chapter which demonstrates that DOUBLETHINK was alive and well when they wrote this bizarre book.

## Genesis 11: The Tower of Babel, and a Quick and Dirty Fix to the Language Thing

*"Coffee is a language in itself." –Jackie Chan.*

Now we come to another of those wonderful contradictions for which the bible has become so famous. After casually informing us of all these wondrous languages seemingly springing out of nowhere in Gen Ten, it seems that Gen Eleven completely contradicts itself: *"Now the whole world had one language and common speech"* (Gen. 11:1). Right off the bat, one language, just ignore all that crap we wrote before, oh wow, look at that blue dog! Meh, whatever; I think that by now, my dearest and beloved book purchasers, you have come to recognize these incongruences like an old friend you might bump into at your mate's weekend party you were invited to and didn't even realize your mate knew this friend of yours too, and the world gets that little bit smaller for the fact.

Where was I? Ah yes, the tower. So a group of peeps who found themselves settled on the Shinar plains get together and think, *"We'll bake some bricks and make ourselves a city"*, with a big-arse tower in the guts of it that *"reaches to the heavens, so that we may make a name for ourselves; otherwise we will be scattered over the face of the whole earth"* (Gen. 11:2 – 11:5). And things were going pretty well, too, by all accounts. But an edifice of that size would not escape the attention of the omnipresent for very long. It then transpired that *"the lord came down to see the city and the tower the people were building"* (Gen. 11:5). Obviously, God saw this as a threat, for he went on record as saying, *"If as one people speaking the same language they have begun to do this, then nothing they plan to do will be impossible for them. Come, let us go down and confuse their language so they will not understand each other"* (Gen. 11:6 – 11:7).

Again, who was God talking to? He'd removed himself from the affairs of humans, washed his hands of the whole bloody mess, and with Noah no longer in the picture, who in the world would have had God's confidences? It couldn't be a human, because backing this course of action would be essentially betraying one's own species. You could argue God's angels/team members/dwarf guards, which would seem reasonable, wherever they happen to be holed up since the flood. The fact that the Tower of Babel was supposed to reach up to heaven would suggest that God (Team Leader Yaweh) had completed sufficient repairs to his ship to establish a low orbit, but not quite enough to finally leave this miserable rock. Hence the suggestion to swoop down (perhaps in some sort of scouting- or fighter-shuttle) to destroy the tower before these humans got too cocky. So the lord *"scattered them from there all over the earth, and they stopped building the city"* (Gen.

11:8). Scattered them, how? The tower itself was undoubtedly destroyed: this assumption is supported by the fact that a) it doesn't exist today, unlike other structures such as the pyramids; and b) the fate of the tower is represented by the Blasted Tower card of any decent Tarot deck, a tale no doubt handed down over the generations of man showing that, despite the scrambling of language, a picture speaks a thousand words, and that the passing down of events will find a way.

I'm guessing the people weren't scattered as a result of the destruction of the tower. The force of the explosion required to scatter the tower to the ends of the earth would have instantly turned any nearby workers into a fine red paste (the soldiers in Vietnam had a term for what remained of those unfortunates who rather carelessly stepped on hidden landmines: goop. Undoubtedly the same principles of corporeal emulsification would apply to whatever weapons God had at his disposal). The other option available would be by forcible abduction and relocation, which might also explain the scrambling of their language. As the people were abducted and relocated, they may have been exposed to just enough focused brain trauma to damage their speech centres; not enough to cause permanent damage, but just enough to wipe all knowledge of language from their minds. And when the relocation was complete, a new language would naturally evolve as those people relearned how to communicate their ideas amongst themselves. This seems the most reasonable assumption to arrive at to explain this story, beyond the ramblings of a demented author.

**From Shem to Abram: it wasn't just language that was scrambled**

So now we're treated to an account of Shem's family line. When Shem was 100 years old, he became the father of Arphaxad. This poses some problems for our Lunar Month theory of time reckoning, because if this is indeed the case, Shem was just over seven-and-a-half years old when he fathered his first son (Gen. 11:10). He then lived another 500 years (essentially, 38 years), fathering other offspring. Now here is the interesting part: When Arphaxad was 35 years of age, he fathered his own son, Shelah. Now, is that Lunar or actual years? The lunar conversion makes Arphaxad two-and-a-half years old when he fathered Shelah, which couldn't possibly be true. Then he punches out another 403 years (31) in a messy twist of temporal mathematics. Shelah himself had a child at thirty (no more than two-and-a-half himself) before living another 403 years.

It's hard to credit these numbers with any measure of authenticity, being all over the shop without rhyme nor reason. We may have to right this section of the bible off as a bad joke, created probably as a result of a brain-scrambling-gone-wrong, which is disappointing not only for the amusement value derived from the improbability of a two-year-old father, but from the author, and subsequently those charming individuals who interrupt your Sunday morning lie-in, trying to convince us that the record is accurate, that the math works, and that you'll go to hell if you don't believe every single word of it. Hmm.

The line of Shem, then, is thus:

| **Name** | **Age at 1st Child** | **Age at Death** |
|---|---|---|
| Shem | 100 (Arphaxad) | 500 |
| Arphaxad | 35 (Shelah) | 403 |
| Shelah | 30 (Eber) | 403 |
| Eber | 34 (Peleg) | 430 |
| Peleg | 30 (Reu) | 209 |
| Reu | 32 (Serug) | 207 |
| Serug | 30 (Nahor) | 200 |
| Nahor | 29 (Terah) | 119 |
| Terah | 70 (Abram, Nahor, Haran) | 205 |

## They're eerie and in-breedy: The Abram's Family

Pretty boring stuff, actually. Terah had Abram, Nahor and Haran, and ultimately Haran died while Terah was still alive, but before that time managed to whelp a young lad with the unlikely name of Lot. Abram married Sarai but remained childless, whilst Nahor married Milkah, who was actually Haran's daughter and his own niece (Gen. 11:29 - way to keep it in the family, pervert). So Terah, for reasons which remain unknown, took Abram, Sarai and Grandchild Lot and headed off for Canaan, however they only got as far as Harran (how wonderfully close to the name Haran) before settling there instead, where Terah eventually died.

Well, I did tell you it was boring stuff. But I include it just to maintain a sense of continuity with the family lines as represented, so that you, the reader, can follow along as accurately as possible. Besides, we cover a lot of biblical ground where Abram and Sarai are concerned, so it's important to make it clear that the acts of lunacy that ensued can be rightly traced to some queer genetic anomalies caused by in-breeding. It's good to know one's family roots, although probably not that intimately.

## Genesis 12: God commits Real Estate Fraud

*"There are three things in the world that deserve no mercy: hypocrisy, fraud and tyranny." –Frederick William Robertson.*

In this gripping chapter, it appears that God just can't keep his nose out of humanity's business, despite the disappointment and floods and heartache and dodgy decision-making that has been the hallmark of his tenure as Supreme Being of the Universe. God turns up in Harran and implores Abram to *"go from your country, your people and your father's household to the land I will show you"* (Gen. 12:1). He then promises to make him into a great nation, and bless him (Gen. 12:2).

It all sounds pretty familiar, doesn't it? Go here, do this, don't eat that, build this, gather that, settle here, get turfed out over there, move to here, et al. I wonder if, at this stage of the game when the flood and even Applegate were recent histories, whether Abram was at all dubious about God's intentions? Then again, he may not have been dubious at all: perhaps in addition to scrambling the speech centres of humankind's brain through their forced relocation, he also wiped their memories of these unpleasant events. Nobody really knows, nor will we ever know. And it doesn't matter, really, because Abram is in front of the big guy right now (well, right then) and of course he would follow the directions of his god. He gathered up his wife, nephew, all his possessions and all the people he had acquired in Harran (acquired people? Servants and slaves, perhaps, or merely acquaintances and well-wishers?) and set off for Canaan (Gen. 12:5). The trip continued through this land *"as far as the great tree of Moreh at Shechem"* (Gen. 12:6), a land currently occupied by the Canaanites (logical assumption, considering they've travelled to a city called Canaan, and cities as a general rule-of-thumb tend to have people living in them).

Then God appeared to Abram and said, *"To your offspring I will give this land"* (Gen. 12:7). So, not only has God *not* wiped his hands of humankind, he's also doing dodgy real estate deals. This is Air-BNB all over again, just barging in and usurping someone else's home, then transferring the ownership to a pack of bloody tourists! You have to wonder at this stage what God's motivation is here. He certainly doesn't need the money; he can just blink that into existence if you take the Supreme Being stance, and money would be no good outside of Earth for the Spaceman Scenario. I'm starting to think he's just stirring the pot to cause some trouble between these Canaanites and Abram's tribe to liven things up a bit. Very unethical behaviour for a god, but I suppose you have to do something to entertain yourself occasionally. So anyway, altars were built, then Abram took off to the hills east of Bethel and made camp between there and Ai (Gen. 12:8), slapped up another altar, then took off toward the Negev (Gen. 12:9).

## Abram in Egypt: The Phooling of the Pharaoh

*"The petty man is eager to make boasts, yet desires that others should believe in him. He enthusiastically engages in deception, yet wants others to have affection for him. He conducts himself like an animal, yet wants others to think well of him." –Xun Kuang.*

Abram and his intrepid group have by this time trudged through the Negev Desert and have rocked up on the outskirts of Egypt (Gen. 12:10). Apparently there was a severe famine in the land (not really surprising to discover a lack of food in a desert) hence Abram's journey to here. Now that he's trudged all this way, it suddenly occurs to him that his life might be in danger, for he then turns to his wife Sarai and says, *"I know what a beautiful woman you are, and if the Egyptians see you, they'll assume you're my wife, take you and kill me. So we'll say you're my sister, so they'll treat me nice for your sake, and spare my life because of you"* (Gen. 12:11 – 12:13). Seems a little bit self-serving, but we'll run with it for now, and return to it shortly. So they descend into Egypt, and the Egyptians indeed find her very appealing; but then the Pharaoh's officials spotted her and as a result they were summarily bundled off to the palace (Gen. 12:15). The Pharaoh was so impressed he bought Sarai for the usual dowry of sheep, camels, servants et al, and was treated well for her sake (so far, so good, notwithstanding the bigamy). God finds out about this, however, and inflicts some nasty diseases on the pharaoh and his house staff because of it (Gen. 12:17). Abram was dragged into the palace again and asked, "Dude, why didn't you tell me she was your WIFE!? Here, take her and go!" (Gen. 12:18). And thus Abram left Egypt with the skin still on his sorry hide, along with Sarai and all his possessions. (Gen. 12:20).

Surely Abram knew what was likely to happen when he started spruiking his wife off as his sister, although I'm still dubious about why he should think he'd live any longer by doing this. After all, if they're willing to kill him to gain access to his wife, wouldn't those same amoral values apply if she were his sister? Why is killing the husband okay and the brother not? Murder is murder, after all, regardless of the motivation behind it; if one has already rationalized the taking of a life, familial relationships would be a moot point. A chancy game to play with one's life, but Abram comes through it in one piece, and with a misbegotten dowry to boot. Free kick Hawthorn.

## Genesis 13: More dodgy land deals, the group divides

*"Buy land, they're not making it anymore." –Mark Twain.*

So Abram and his party have done pretty well for themselves, heading back to the Negev with his ill-gotten gains and slightly-used wife. Ultimately the group travel back to Abram's altar between Bethel and Ai, and Abram got busy calling on God again (Gen. 13:1 – 13:4).

Abram's nephew Lot was still with them, of course, and had also amassed his own wealth of livestock and servants and tents and whatnot, and was wealthy in his own right by this juncture. Unfortunately the land in which they were currently staying could not support such a host of people and animals, causing in-fighting between Abram's people and Lot's (Gen. 13:7). And so it was decided to part company and seek their fortunes on their own. Lot looked about him and found the plain of Jordan nice and well-watered, fancied it looked a bit like the garden of Eden (how he arrived at this comparison when Eden had been shut off for centuries is unclear) and chose that path (Gen. 13:10).

Abram pushed off toward Canaan, whilst Lot chose a nice cosy spot just outside of Sodom. When he'd done this and both companies were more or less settled, God took Abram aside and, in another dodgy land deal, said, *"Look around from where you are, to the north and south, to the east and west. All the land that you see I will give to you and your offspring forever"* (Gen. 13:14 – 13:15). So Abram pitched tents and built yet another altar near the trees of Mamre at Hebron (Gen. 13:18).

You know, readers, with all this land just being given away, I'm left wondering how the recipients of that land are going about proving they own it. It's all very well for God to be giving away this desert or that plain, but it's only word-of-mouth, isn't it, and always discussed with just the one person, the one wanting the land in the first place. Where are the papers, the bills of sale? Even a scrap of parchment saying I, God, hereby give this tract of land to Abram forever, amen? Any disputes over ownership would quickly be resolved by that simple expedient, because who wants to get into a war over land when you have a deity ready to defend the rightful owner? And it allows the displaced people already on the land to lodge a grievance with God at their nearest altar (all prayers to be lodged in triplicate, three months in advance, please..). It would seem that the taking of land by alleged Divine Right is alive and well, and so early in the game, too. Fortune, as ever, favours the brave.

## Genesis 14: Abram Saves Lot's arse, deals with kings

This is one of the more pedantic verses of the bible, and I apologize for including it, but if we're to do a modern interpretation of this thing, then we need to plough through it. Essentially, there are a whole bunch of kings in the area; self-proclaimed, most likely, because I'm pretty sure democracy wasn't a thing yet, which would make the title of "King" redundant. A few opportunistic but no doubt charismatic individuals stepped up and assumed authority by the likely expedients of family ties with recent history's notable personages (Adam, Noah, et al). Whatever the reason, they've proclaimed themselves kings and helped themselves to the lion's share of the current wealth of the land through birthright.

A group of these kings got together with their forces, and organized a rebellion against some other leader's oppression in the Valley of Siddim. Apparently during this rebellion, the Kings of Sodom and Gomorrah were routed, and in the process of the people fleeing, some happened to run into the tar pits situated in that Valley and met their demise. Okay, I can't really see why it was necessary to add this to the story, but we'll run with it. It should also be pretty easy to determine if this happened by the exhumation of their bodies from the pits. After all, tar is such a wonderful preservative, a fact the Egyptians were aware of because they used it to coat the bodies of their deceased royalty as part of the mummification process. And even if they're just bones by now (the sinking of a trapped animal, for instance, could take months, by which time extensive decomposition would have occurred) they should still be there and able to be accurately carbon-dated to verify these events. I look forward to the expedition.

Okay, so the Sodom and Gomorrah kings were routed, and the victors took their fill of goods, foodstuffs and people, including the hapless Lot, who happened to be in the city at the time (Gen. 14:11 – 14:12). When word of this reached Abram's ear, he gathered up his own forces (318 men born of his own household), tracked down those responsible, and subsequently defeated them, recovering *"all the goods and brought back Lot and his possessions, together with the women and the other people"* (Gen. 14:16). Not many generals of armies can boast a 100% mission success rate (Rescue the Relative, Save the People, Recover the Things), but Abram manages to do this without the benefit of a battle plan, making it up as he goes, without loss. It probably helped that he attacked this group at night, taking them unawares in their sleep, but even then you would expect some loss of life, or at least goods, or the very least the taking of the women as battle spoils. These things happen in war, and yet Abram dodged all these foibles of the fighting army. Well played, I guess.

After returning from his resounding victory, Abram is approached by the king of Sodom in the valley of Shaveh (coined King's Valley). Then the king of Salem rocks up to the meeting and, being *"a priest of God Most High"*, starts praising Abram, saying, *"Blessed be Abram by God Most High, creator of heaven and earth"* (Gen. 14:18 – 14:20). Then for some reason, Abram gives this guy a tenth of everything (Gen. 14:21). Er, why…? Glancing back over the entirety of Gen. 14, there is no mention of this Melchizedek king of Salem anywhere in the passage (nor is this guy mentioned in any previous passages, for that matter) until he rocks up after all the fighting has finished, hands around some crusty bread and a some plonk, and ends up with a tenth of everything Abram "owns" (I say "owns" for simplicity's sake, because the whole "God gave it to me" argument distracts us from the issue at hand, which is confusing enough as it is without debating the legalities).

The king of Sodom simply implores Abram to give the people back, and to keep whatever goods recovered for himself (Gen. 14:21). But Abram refuses, saying, *"With raised hand I have sworn an oath to the lord, God Most High, blah blah-blah, that I will accept nothing belonging to you, not even a thread or the strap of a sandal, so that you will never be able to say, 'I made Abram rich.'"*, instead letting his co-generals Aner, Eshkol and Mamre have their share (Gen. 14:22 – 14:24).

When did that particular agreement happen? Abram had nothing to do with the king of Sodom prior to his rescuing of his nephew Lot. We know (by being told, naturally) that Sodom was a den of iniquity, although Abram was unlikely to be aware of this, having gone west away from the place, because his nephew Lot had chosen the area for his own tribe. And a young man is less-than-forthcoming with uncomfortable facts to his uncle as a general rule, especially one who has taken on the role of Father-figure after Lot's own father kicked the bucket and orphaned him. Had Abram known about Lot's parking up next to the biblical equivalent of Las Vegas, words would surely have been exchanged, and not pleasant ones, either.

In fact, the only appearance God made to Abram that is recorded is when they parted their ways and God was handing out those dodgy real estate deals. No mention of, "Hey Abram, did you know that your nephew's living near Sin City?", or perhaps, "Abe, buddy, if you ever run into some guy who claims to be the king of Sodom, be sure not to accept anything from him because he'll hold it over your arse, he's just that kinda guy, 'kay..''? Because, as this bible is supposed to be the Life and Times of The Big Guy, you would think it would have been mentioned in there at some stage. Or there's the chance that Abram didn't like the look of the guy and evoked some mysterious prior promise to God not accept any largesse to avoid having to deal with the man in the future. Either-or.

## Genesis 15: God experiments with interactive holographic communication

On the subject of pow-wows with immortal beings, it seems God has found a new novel way of manipulating his favourite followers, for *"the word of the Lord came to Abram in a vision: 'Do not be afraid, Abram. I am your shield, your very great reward.'"* (Gen. 15:1). Not coming to his people personally anymore, but in a "vision". And why would God have to implore Abram not to be afraid? After all, Abe and the Big Guy have been kicking back and talking and making plans for Abram for quite a while now, so it's not as if God's presence was entirely unexpected; you could understand the apprehension if God suddenly appeared to you while you were out shopping or doing the laundry, or batting one off while watching the women's super-netball on the weekend (feel free to change the gender and/or activity to suit your own personal inclinations). Perhaps then, the cause of Abram's fear is that God is there, but not *really* there. God is being described as a "vision," which would imply a visible aspect to the presence while being simultaneously incorporeal, when up until now any interactions with God have been in a more tangible fashion.

Perhaps God has been able to create one of those cool robot doctors they have in some hospitals nowadays, controlled by remote and is somewhat mobile, but without the tediousness of actually having to be near the patient? He can just fire up the screen, dole out his instructions/commands and leave without being pestered all the way home with hundreds of tiresome follow-up questions. But if we want to continue properly exploring the extra-terrestrial visitor theory, we could easily conclude that Team Leader Yaweh and his team have finally succeeded in repairing their communications systems, and now instead of the interminable shuttle trips to the surface, God can either send an interactive holographic communication to Abram (along the lines of what we've seen in countless science fiction movies and television series) or, better yet, transport himself down to the planet a 'la Star Trek; although the physics needed to achieve this, not to mention the huge energy requirements and the practical and ethical considerations (send the bits or send the data?), makes this impossible for us at our stage of technological development. For a species that has mastered travel between the stars, however, almost anything is possible, especially if they have been able to develop faster-than-light (FTL) travel or something close enough to it without all the bothersome Newtonian physics getting in the way.

Where was I? Ah yes. Ignoring the shield and reward claims, Abram has overcome his initial fear and is now suddenly asking, *"What can you give me since I remain childless and the one who will inherit my estate is Eliezer of Damascus?"* (Gen. 15:2). *"You have given me no children; so a servant in my household will be my heir."* Okaaay, God's only just dropped in to say hi, and you're already hitting him up for freebies and any spare children he has lying around? Seems a little presumptuous to me, considering all the real estate he's already given the guy despite that real estate being occupied by someone else at the time. As far as the having offspring is concerned, I'm not quite sure Abram has a grip on how procreation works. It's quite possible, as fantastic as that sounds: I personally know someone who was so naïve, she was having sex with her boyfriend/fiancé and, apparently, didn't realise that's what they were doing. This same individual also cut short a date midway through one of these occurrences because she thought she'd wet herself (when really it was …. well, you can draw your own mental imagery here, dear readers, but you may need counselling later). My point is that it is difficult to fathom the average person NOT recognizing the sex act when they see it without a profound head injury or some other severe cognitive disability. The fact is you're either not playing with a full deck, or you're deluding yourself.

Anyway, back to The Birds and The Bees 101. Then the word of the Lord came to Abram again and said, *"This man will not be your heir, but a son who is your own flesh and blood will be your heir"* (Gen. 15:4). Maybe God has one of those "Having Children for Dummies" books lying about the place somewhere, or is passing on a few helpful pointers. Who knows? Abram for his part appears to believe what God's telling him, but still needs some reassurance. So God instructs Abram to gather, *"a heifer, a goat and a ram, all 3 years old, and a dove and a pigeon" (Gen. 15:9).* He gathered the necessary animals and birds, and then *"cut them in two, and arranged the halves opposite each other; the birds he did not cut in half" (Gen. 15:10)*. He kept the birds of prey away from the remains, fell asleep sometime in the afternoon, and had a rather disturbing dream that God told him that his desc-endants will be slaves for the next 400 years, but that he'll die old and peacefully. Furthermore, after the centuries of slavery and abuses, the descendants will emerge rich and bountiful. Then after the sun had set and it was dark, a smoking pot and a torch *"appeared, and passed over the pieces [of animal carcass]" (Gen. 15:11 – 15:19)*. Then God resumed giving away more land that other people had already settled, from the Wadi to the Euphrates (Gen. 15:20), essentially the lands currently occupied by no less than ten different peoples.

So let's go back to the animals. Why is it that every time an animal is asked for, the people involved (in this case Abram) automatically assume they have to kill it or burn it or bifurcate it or in any way violate the poor creature? God could just as easily have wanted to milk the heifer for a refreshing pitcher of milk, the goat to keep the grass in Eden at a reasonable height, and the ram for certain other intensely personal reasons? Perhaps he wanted the dove and the pigeon for backup communications in case their array failed again, but luckily the birds weren't molested in any significant way on this one occasion.

There's not much to examine in regards to Abram falling asleep in the afternoon. He was fatigued from the efforts of violently dividing animals and scaring off scavenger birds, found a nice spot in the sun and had a nanna-nap; and because the issue of progeny was foremost on his mind, it's not surprising that any dreams would contain fanciful scenarios involving any children that might eventuate. I know from my own experience that if you happen to find a nice spot to nap in, you can lose some serious time in dreamland and sometimes wake up feeling like Superman after a kryptonite enema.

The phenomenon of the "smoking pot and the torch" passing over the animal halves is intriguing, but not entirely unexplainable. Another side effect of succumbing to a super-righteous nap, on awakening, is a profound sense of disorientation, which may or may not include that sticky gunk from your eyes that glues them shut. Given that Abram had spent the afternoon dismembering animals in the desert and kicking up dust while chasing off scavenging birds lends possibility to this. And because it was dark when he awoke (being perhaps disoriented and/or gummy in the eyes), it's feasible that he woke to find someone wandering along with a torch and, depending on the person's position relative to the torch, may not have actually been able to see a person carrying it. There are no specific references to "a smoking pot" in Google literature (unless a censer is meant by this obscure wording), however it could just as easily have meant someone actually *smoking pot*, i.e. some blissed-out local enjoying a nice evening spliff after dinner, stumbling onto Abram's offerings, waving the torch over them bemusedly and sagely opining, 'Woooah dude, that's seriously messed up..' before wandering off again. Totally possible. I challenge anyone to prove otherwise.

"Woooahh... that's totally messed up, dude..."

## Genesis 16: Call him Ishmael

*"I have also fantasised myself to be his female slave, but this does not suffice, for after all every woman can be the slave of her husband."* –Richard Von Kraft-Ebing, Psychopathia Sexualis: The Case Histories.

Our latest passage enters on the scene of Abram and Sarai, discussing their childlessness as couples struggling to conceive will often do. But let's add to this the introduction of Sarai's Egyptian slave, Hagar (like Hagar the Horrible, perhaps..?). So in a flash of womanly insight, Sarai says to Abram, *"The lord has kept me from having children. Go, sleep with my slave; perhaps I can build my family through her."* (Gen. 16:2). Abram agreed to what Sarai said (no surprise there!) so after ten years in Canaan Sarai gave her slave Hagar to Abram to be his wife (the dawn of polygamy). Abram got busy with the slave girl, and she conceived. Once Hagar found she was pregnant, she began to despise her mistress Sarai (the dawn of pride). So Sarai went to Abram and said, *"You are responsible for the wrong I am suffering ... May the lord judge between you and me"* (Gen. 16:5).

Um....what?! Although we shouldn't be surprised by this turn events, should we readers? Abram's fallen into the classic trap, and is quickly learning the error of his ways, in that when a woman gives permission for something (especially concerning extramarital sex) it is not *really* permission, and you'd better have your wits about you if you hope to get out of that predicament alive and with your genitalia intact.

I've had this myself, although not with anything as remotely scintillating as extramarital sex (although while there's life, there's hope..!). Nay, mine was with a big boofhead of a dog that wasn't getting the attention it needed by the family (I'm not a dog person by nature, and this furry horse was brought home despite my specific objections, i.e. nobody will look after it). But I digress. It was impressed on the family that it needed walking, and preparations were made between (then) wife and daughter to walk this dog. I was watching on and, predicting the future slightly, said, "You're going to have to tighten that collar or it'll get loose…" Cue forward about one minute and, true to prediction, once outside the front gate the dog reversed itself, dug in against the leash, slipped the collar and bolted off down the street. First reaction: "Oh, GOOD one, Steve!!" despite being nowhere near the action. Ah, families are great, aren't they?

Anyway, back to the story: Abram finds himself in this nasty little space, where Sarai has sanctioned his sleeping with the slave girl to create a family, but then when this actually happens, it's all Abram's fault. Classic rookie mistake right there, Abe. Thankfully he isn't wearing any of it, and says, *"The slave is in your hands, do with her what you think best." (Gen. 16:6).* Abe has got his wits about him, claiming that it's still Sarai's slave and therefore hers to discipline as she sees fit, despite marrying the slave girl and ipso-facto having claim to responsibility for her in his own right (Gen. 16:3); a great recovery from what could've been a no-win situation.

Sarai, for her part, takes this on board and subsequently goes to town on the uppity slave girl as only a jealous, barren wife is capable; Hagar takes the hint and absconds into the desert. It transpires that one of God's angels finds her parked up next to a spring in the desert, and asks, *"Hagar slave of Sarai, where have you come from and where are you going?"* (Gen. 16:8).

"I'm running away from my mistress, Sarai."

The angel then commands, *"Go back to your mistress and submit to her. You're pregnant and (besides promising her progeny too numerous to count) will give birth to a son. You'll call him Ishmael because the lord has heard of your misery."* He rants on to say that Ishmael be a wild donkey of a man, raising his hand to all others, living in hostility against all his brothers, and generally being a prick of a thing. Anyway,

Hagar bore this wild donkey-son when Abram was eighty-six, and there endeth Genesis 16.

A couple of things. Assuming God is omnipresent, you would have to think that this omnipresence would filter down somewhat to his angels, who are also immortal and are for all intents and purposes his lieutenants; hired muscle, if you will. Why then would this particular angel ask Hagar where she was from and where she was going? Doesn't he know already? If God is taking such a vested interest in Abram and his getting of progeny, surely everybody would be aware of the situation, a fact that's reinforced by this angel addressing Hagar by name AND knowing where she came from, ie. Abram's camp.

Secondly, this angel then says that God is aware of her misery. A self-inflicted, utterly deserved misery if you ask me: if she hadn't got all high-and-mighty with Sarai in the fact that she could get pregnant where her mistress could not, to her mistress's husband, and with her blessing no less, you have to draw the conclusion that she deserved to get her arse kicked for being such an uppity cow. And yet God seems to be taking the slave's side over Sarai's, whose only fault was infertility (and, perhaps, letting Abram get busy with the Hagar in the first place). But as yet there are no commandments written in stone (Thou Shalt Not Jiggy

Thy Wife's Slave didn't make the top ten, apparently) there's not much God can do in the smiting department but let it ride and promise Hagar more kids to look after.

## Genesis 17: You want me to do WHAT...?!?!?!?!

*"Creator of the universe went to great trouble to create the foreskin. Then insisted that you cut it off. Makes sense." –Richard Dawkins, via Twitter.*

We start this chapter with Abram now ninety years old, when God appeared to him and says, *"I am God almighty; walk before me faithfully and be blameless" (Gen. 17:1)*. After Abram does all his ritual groveling in the dirt, God then says, *"From now on, you will be called Abraham; you'll be fruitful, you will father many nations, and many kings will come from you"* (Gen. 17:4 -17:5). He goes on about more covenants of this nature, and says that *"the whole land of Canaan, where you now reside as a foreigner, I will give as an everlasting possession to you and your descendants, and I will be their God"* (Gen. 17:8).

Wait a minute.... Wasn't Canaan already promised to Abraham (nee Abram) in Geneses (Genesises?) 12:7 *and* 13:4)? A bit of triple-redundancy going on here, unless he needs to update his documentation to reflect his deity-enforced name change. It's such a pain in the arse if you don't get things like names right; get it wrong here and you'll end up in Centrelink for the rest of your life trying to convince mindless, embittered bureaucrats of the authenticity of yourself and your claim.

But never mind that for now. God reiterates these promises, and then things take a very unexpected turn for the ugly. You may like to check out the wording of Genesis 17 for yourselves, dear readers, but I very much doubt it went quite as smoothly at that. To my rather hyperactive imagination, the following interpretation might be a little closer to the truth:

God: So Abe, buddy, how goes it?

Abraham: Okay for an old bugger. The new name's gonna take time to adapt to, though! So what can I do ya for, G-man?

God: Good news: I'm giving you all of the lands of Canaan.

Abraham: Well, thanks for that, lord, but didn't you already promise me that land, back when Lot and I parted ways on the hill, before that thing with the Pharaoh?

G: Oh yeah, of course, duh..! Well, it really IS yours now, and to make it official, I'll establish my covenant with you on it.

Abraham: Oh..! You mean like that promise-thing you made with my great-great-great-great-great-great-great-great grandfather Noah with the rainbow? That sounds pretty cool! Do I get a rainbow too?

G: Weeellll, not as such. Not a rainbow, as such…

Abe: Oh… okay then, what are we talking about here?

G: My covenant with you is that every male among you shall be circumcised.

Abe: What's that, like a special tattoo or something?

[God tells him]

Abe: [blinks, once] Say what..?

[God tells him again]

Abe: You're serious?

G: That is my covenant.

Abe: You want me to take out my penis…

G: Yes..

Abe: …grab a razor-sharp knife…

G: Uh-huh..

Abe: …and slice the tip off. Actually cut it off. With a knife.

G: Pretty much. But it's not the tip, Abe, it's just that flappy bit covering the tip. I don't like it.

Abe: Okay, quick question: Are you FUCKING CRAZY!?!??!

G: Abe, chill. It's just a bit of skin, you don't need it. And anyway, it looks ugly and it's all I can smell when I visit. You should really wash more, Abe, but you're in the middle of the desert so I figure this is the next best thing.

Seriously, it's worse than the time I left my limburger cheese in the conservatory last summer...

Abe: YOU GIVE THAT MENTAL DRUNK BASTARD NOAH A RAINBOW AS A COVENANT, AND MINE IS TO HACK OFF MY JUNK?!! WHAT THE FUCK IS WRONG WITH YOU?!??! Oh my fucking GOD!!!....

G: [looking a little nonplussed] I'm right here, Abe...

Abe: [unabashed] That's harsh, man, so harsh. How *exactly* do you expect me to get everyone on board with this?! It's not like I'm implementing a clean-shaven policy, you know..! You want me to slice up their skin flutes!! Totes inappropes, dude...!!

G: I'm sure you'll find a way. Promise them goat-wives or something, I dunno. Be creative.

Abe: What if I don't want to do this?

G: Then I'll send you to hell and you'll suffer torture and pain.

Abe: You want me to cut my own dick with a knife, G. I fail to see the threat.

G: In hell, the pain lasts over and over forever.

Abe: Touché...

G: Abe, relax. No pain, no gain, right..? [cackles insanely]

Abe: I'm seriously worried about you, G…

G: Oh, and your wife's name is Sarah now…

[Abe facepalms.]

A few more things before we move on. If man was indeed created in God's image, why does he now want to change that image? Furthermore, if foreskins bothered him that much, why put one on Adam in the first place? And now because of that oversight, mankind is expected to make it right with some self-inflicted cosmetic surgery? Also, how is Sarai's forced name change going to affect her fertility in any significant way?

As far as the practice of circumcision is concerned in today's world, I will only offer the following observations, and I will leave it up to you to either agree or disagree, as is your right as loyal book-purchasers. Firstly, while some may argue that this practice is unnecessary, barbaric or cruel, there are some practical benefits outside the tenets of religion. If it is done at all, it is usually performed when the child is a week old, and while it is no doubt painful, it is never remembered as most people do not recall events earlier than four years old, perhaps two if a person is especially eidetic. Secondly, the women I have spoken to over my life have universally reported that urinary tract infections are virtually non-existent with circumcised males as compared with their noncircumcised counterparts, owing to the foreskin's penchant for trapping moisture and inviting the growth of some nasty things, especially in countries with a hot climate. Thirdly, women also report that circumcised men last, on average, much longer in sexual congress than uncircumcised men; this is probably due to the desensitization of nerve endings in the glans that are normally protected by the foreskin. And from what I've been told of such things, women much prefer their partners to last two-and-a-half hours, rather than two-and-a-half thrusts. Finally, there are certain medical conditions (paraphimosis in particular) that can result in an emergency circumcision being necessary to prevent irreparable damage to the penis. And I presume to speak for all males everywhere when I say that if this procedure needs to be done, I would much prefer it done when I'm a week old and won't remember it than to suffer through that kind of pain as an adult, in an emergency situation. I'm sure the guy I know for whom this happened just recently would agree wholeheartedly on this point.

Finally, proof-positive that God has a sense of humour in Gen. 17:14: *"Any uncircumcised male, which has not been circumcised in the flesh, will be cut off from his people."* Good one, God, thy one-liners are as good as thy jests...!

## Genesis 18: Sarah finds God funny, Abraham pushes Shit Uphill

*"Man is an animal that makes bargains: no other animal does this – no dog exchanges bones with another." –Adam Smith.*

An initially boring passage, where God and three of his mates happened to wander past Abraham's tent and were subsequently implored to share a meal with him. When they acquiesced, Abe told his wife Sarah to *"quickly bake some bread"* (Gen. 18:6), while he ran off to find a nice calf to slaughter and eat, all of which probably took an hour or two to prepare and serve, if starting from scratch. So for an impromptu invitation, these guys are quite patient. When they had finally got around to eating, one of the guys asked where Abe's wife Sarah was, and Abe indicated she was in the tent. When one guy indicated that *"I will surely return to you about this time next year, and Sarah your wife will have a son" (Gen. 18:10)*. Sarah, in the tent, heard this statement and thought it was highly amusing considering their advanced ages (unquantified, however Abe was ninety-nine years old when he self-mutilated). We shall assume solar years here, because 99 lunar years would make him seven-and-a-half solar years old, which seems highly unlikely given the adventures Abe has already enjoyed.

God hears the laughter and is all, "Why did Sarah laugh and say, 'Will I really have a child, now that I am old?'" (Gen. 18:13). Sarah lied about laughing, but God's all like, "Actually, you did." See, nothing interesting, just Sarah getting caught out in a lie, but with no apparent retribution or smiting or anything like that (yet). Boring.

Onward to part two. God and his mates have eaten their fill and are preparing to leave. They have a decent view of Sodom from where they're standing, and God asks his buddies, *"Shall I hide from Abraham what I am about to do?" (Gen. 18:17)*. Referring, of course, being the destruction of Sodom due to the wickedness and iniquity into which it has degenerated. The very iniquity that was supposed to have been washed away with that flood, remember? Oh well; like any cancer, if you don't kill it all, it has a habit of growing back. God then says that, *"The outcry against Sodom and Gomorrah is so great and their sin so grievous that I will go down and see if what they've done is as bad as the outcry that has reached me." (Gen. 18:21)*. So God is learning some diplomacy; rather than just smite them out-of-hand, he's going to personally inspect the place to verify the claims, and act accordingly. Damned decent of the deity, if you ask me.

Of course, Abe gets wind of God's plans for the two cities, and asks, *"Will you sweep away the righteous with the wicked? What if there are fifty righteous people there, will you sweep it away and not spare the place for the sake of those fifty righteous people?" (Gen. 18:22 on.)* Then he tries to take the moral high ground with the Creator: *"Far be it from you to do such a thing – to kill the righteous with the wicked, treating the wicked and righteous alike!"* Hmm. He seems to have forgotten the whole Flood saga, methinks, or he wouldn't be making such a statement.

He seems to have caught God on a good day, however, for he replies, *"If I find fifty righteous people in the city of Sodom, I will spare the whole place for their sake." (Gen. 18:26).* Emboldened by this caveat, Abe presses his luck.

Abe: What about for five less than fifty? Will you kill them all for the lack of five short of fifty?

G: Okay, if I find 45 people, I won't destroy Sodom.

Abe: What if you only find forty..?

G: Okay, if I find 40 people, I won't destroy it.

Abe: What about thirty…?

G: [sighs] Really..? Okay, if I find thirty, Sodom won't be destroyed.

Abe: What about twenty?

G: What about it? Okay Abe, if I find twenty righteous people, I won't destroy the place.

Abe: What about ten?

G: Abe, you're pissing me off now. Okay fine, if I find ten, I won't destroy Sodom.

Apparently, they got bored with haggling at this point and they went home. Which teaches us an important lesson: If you want to destroy a city because you think it's evil, the acceptable limit of innocent casualties is ten.

## Genesis 19: Sodom and Gomorrah: cities that are so camp, they're made with tents

*"From a religious point of view, if God had thought homosexuality is a sin, he would not have created gay people."* –Howard Dean.

Two angels arrive at Sodom in the evening, to be greeted by Lot who was skulking about the city gates. He does his ritual groveling and then implores the pair to *"turn aside to your servant's house. You can wash your feet and spend the night and then go on your way early in the morning."* (Gen. 19:2). They replied in the negative, wanting to spend the night in the city square. Lot insisted so strongly on this that the angels demurred and entered Lot's house, where they were treated to flat bread. So far, so good, I suppose.

Shortly thereafter, every man from every party of the city – young and old – came to Lot's door and called, *"Where are the men who came to you tonight? Bring them out to us so that we can have sex with them"* (Gen. 9:5). Lot went out and guarded his door, imploring the crowd not to do this, instead saying, *"Look, I have two daughters who have never slept with a man. Let me bring them out to you, and you can do what you like with them. But don't do anything to these men, for they have come under the protection of my roof"* (Gen. 19:8). What a charming father he must be, whoring out his daughters to a sex-crazed crowd! Luckily, the daughters are in no immediate danger, thanks to Lot's fundamental misunderstanding of the sexual desires of the mob at his door.

As Lot baulked the crowd, they started forward intending to break down his door, but the two men inside (MEN now, not ANGELS) reached out and dragged Lot inside; after which, the two MEN *"struck the men who were at the door of the house, young and old, with blindness so that they could not find the door." (Gen. 19:11)*. Striking them with blindness is a pretty neat trick, and I'd like to know how they did that. But honestly, a door is a rather large thing to lose, particularly if you're standing right in front of it at the time. It's just a matter of smacking yourself into the wall and then feeling your way toward the door. The only problem I could envisage for these blinded fruitbats is their ability to locate the two angels/men once inside the house, and then subduing them sufficiently to allow molestation to occur.

The two guys/angels then turn to Lot and ask him if he has other wives/daughters/relatives in the city, and if so to get them out of town fast, *"because we are going to destroy this place. The outcry to the lord against its people is so great that he has sent us to destroy it." (Gen. 19:13)*. A fair call, I say: If I went to a town and every male in the place tried to forcibly enter my exit, I'd probably put a flamethrower to the joint and everyone in it, too.

I should point out right here that I don't particularly care if a guy prefers guys, girls, goats or whatever other sexual preference they have. It's their life, and their choice after all. In fact I have a number of friends who prefer their own gender. The only time it becomes objectionable is if they choose to rub that choice in your face, and then get all upset if you react. A person can be gay, lesbian, bisexual, whatever, and still behave like any other person on the planet. There is absolutely no reason to employ exaggerated lisping or "flaming", except to draw attention to yourself and get in peoples' faces. If you're gay, fine, great: I don't need to know your gender preferences, and if you DO want to ask someone for sex, then the mature approach is probably your best chance of success if the other person is similarly inclined, and of minimizing any affront if they're not. Just act naturally, okay? Acting out extrovertly comes across as artificial and immature, and you're unlikely to have a lasting, meaningful relationship with anyone if you're too busy making it all about you.

Now that we have that straightened out (pun intended), we'll return to the scene before us. After the men/angels ask about any relatives in the city, Lot then goes out (into the sex-crazed mob, of course) and spoke to his future sons-in-law and asked them to leave, that the lord was going to destroy the city. The sons-in-law thought he was joking and did not believe him (Gen. 19:14). Question: If *"every man from every part of the city" (Gen. 9:5)* were at Lot's door trying to forcibly rape these angels/men, would that not include Lot's sons-in-law? They were males, yes? If so, they wouldn't have been too hard to find; and secondly, who would want sons-in-law in the family who have been blinded for wanting to rape other men?

The angels by this stage were running out of patience, for they told Lot to grab his family and flee before dawn, lest they be destroyed with the city, and when Lot hesitated, these angels grabbed him, his wife and two daughters, and led them from the city (Gen. 19:15 – 19:16). Once clear of the city, the angels (see, angels again, not men) told them to flee for the mountains, to not look back, and not stop anywhere on the plain; But Lot pleaded again, saying he would never outrun the blast, and suggested he shelter in a small town nearby (named Zoar). The angels agreed to this, and said, *"flee quickly, because I cannot do anything until you reach it (Gen. 19:22).* Why the town is called Zoar for this reason is beyond me, but I imagine Zoar has some archaic Hebrew meaning which translates as, "Place To Which You Flee To Avoid The Holocaust Of Sodom

Because It Was Evil And Must Be Punished With Fire". Additionally, why the angels could not act until Lot reached this town is unknown, as they were going to torch Sodom with everyone in it anyway, until Lot fed them. Perhaps updated orders from God were involved. Anyway, they reached this Zoar, God opened a can of whoop-ass on Sodom, and razed the place with a rain of sulphur (Gen. 19:24). Lot's wife, however, looked back and was turned into a pillar of salt.

It's not clear whether Lot's wife was being punished for seeing God at work or whether she was just caught up in the immolation. Neither is it made clear whether she was turned into a complete pillar of salt or whether she was just coated with it as a byproduct of the sulphur storm descending on Sodom. The interesting thing is that the biblical fire-and-brimstone smells a lot like sulphur. Coincidence? Or are we looking at a God turning to the Dark Side of the force? Is God and Satan (whom we've not seen referred to in the bible yet) the same person? We're supposed to believe that the Father, Son and Holy Ghost are all one and the same person; if we're going to believe this as we're expected to believe the invisible man in the sky, is it really that far a stretch of the imagination to suggest that God and Satan are the same entity, merely two sides of the same coin? The original Harvey Two-Face, perhaps?

One thing is for certain: even today, nothing will grow on the site where Sodom was supposed to have stood. It's the type of barren wasteland one might expect from a biological or thermal weapon or a nuclear blast, assuming either of those can replicate a fire-and-brimstone appearance and smell. For a space-faring species, these things are equally possible, and it would certainly ensure that no upstart humans make further inappropriate sexual demands of the gods.

One other, minor niggly point of order before we continue. In Gen. 18:21 God specifically said that HE would go down and see for himself the iniquity and depravity of Sodom, and yet he sends two of his flunkies instead. Call me pedantic if you will, but if someone says they're going to go and see a thing, I kind of expect them to follow through with that, not send a couple of hired lackeys to see it and report back. Yes, yes, you could argue that God saw through the angels/men's eyes, but he could easily have done that through mortal man's eyes without the need to send his winged goons. And that's not entertaining the long-held belief that God is omnipresent and sees everything, everywhere, at any time. An interesting argument to throw at your next Jehovah's Witnesses or similar religious Sunday Visitors when they say that God kills a puppy every time you self-pleasure.

### Part II: Lot keeps it in the Family

Shortly after this destruction of the evil Sodom, Lot and his daughters left Zoar for fear of staying there, and headed to the mountains to live in a cave. Lot's daughters weren't terribly pleased with this arrangement, as there were no men in the area with whom to get married and procreate as was their wont. So older and younger daughter contrived between themselves to get their ageing father drunk with wine and, on successive nights, took turns to sleep with him and conceived a child each. (Gen. 19:31 – 19:36). These sons (Moab and Ammon) spawned Moabites and Ammonites respectively.

I have a major problem with this. On both occasions, Lot was *"not aware of it when she lay down or when she got up" (Gen. 19:33 and 19:35)*. Perhaps the alcohol of the day affected humans differently, but I can tell you right now I have NEVER drunk so much that I've been unable to remember sleeping with someone, and beyond a certain level of inebriation you're unlikely to get it up at all (see: Brewer's Droop). Furthermore, it's said that the daughters "lay down" on both occasions. With Christianity's insistence on the Missionary Position as the only sanctioned method of intercourse between male and female, it's very unlikely Lot would have been unaware of the physical need of getting on top, so to speak. And if it's the daughters who have climbed aboard, you again have the issue of pushing rope from excessive alcohol consumption, otherwise you're pretty much guaranteed that Lot was aware of everything that was happening. And if by some minor miracle he was blissfully unaware of both nights, he would have to question how his daughters got pregnant in the mountains with no males nearby for his daughters to couple with. Occam's Razor suggests awareness and, from the resulting pregnancies, enjoyment.

## Genesis 20: Abe's up to his old shit again

*"Those that don't learn from their mistakes are doomed to repeat them." –George Santayana.*

We catch up with Abraham in this passage moving on from his digs near Sodom back to the region of the Negev, settling between Kadesh and Shur. He abided in Gerar for a while, and started spruiking his wife off as his sister again (Gen. 20:2), which prompted the King Abimelek of Gerar to send for Sarah and subsequently take her. God, of course, wasn't wearing any of this because he apparently came to the Abimelek in a dream and said, *"You are as good as dead because of the woman you have taken; she is a married woman." Gen. 20:3).* Abimelek, however, had merely taken Sarah at this stage, not consummated her. He did rather baulk at this dream, saying *"Did he not say to me, 'She is my sister,' and didn't she also say, 'He is my brother'?" (Gen. 20:5).* God replied that this was the reason he didn't allow the king to touch Sarah, but if she wasn't returned postehaste, there would be trouble.

The next morning, Abimelek summoned his officials and then had Abraham dragged in. *"What have you done to us? How have I wronged you that you have brought such great guilt upon me and my kingdom?" (Gen. 20:9).* When asked why he did this, Abraham offered the old "If She Was My Wife You Would Have Killed Me" chestnut as an excuse for again whoring his wife out to the nearest available king. He then further divulges that Sarah is step-sister to him (apparently), so what he said was the truth, after a fashion.

So at the end of this meeting, the god-cursed king rewards Abraham's deception by giving him *"sheep and cattle and male and female slaves, and returned his wife Sarah" (Gen. 20:9)*. He also invited Abraham to live anywhere he liked within his kingdom, and gave him one thousand shekels of silver, *"to cover the offense against Sarah before all who are with her" (Gen. 20:16)*. Then Abraham *"prayed to God, who healed Abimelek and his wife and slaves so that they could have children again" (Gen. 20:17)*.

I'm starting to think that Abraham is half pimp, half extortionist. He whores out his wife to the nearest king time and again, passing her off as his sister; and in exchange for material gain, he uses his hired muscle (i.e. God) to remove any curses, plagues or punishments the king unwittingly incurs by taking Abe's wife for his own. What sort of moral story is this supposed to be teaching the people who read this? To screw over the other person every chance you get? If power corrupts, and absolute power corrupts absolutely, it's no wonder Abraham is strutting around like he's the Godfather of the Holy Mafia! What an unscrupulous arsehole!

## Genesis 21: The Nonagenarian Birth Miracle and the Spurned Mistress

*"Next to the pleasure of finding a new mistress is that of being rid of an old one." –William Wycherley.*

Despite Sarah's amoral partnership with Abraham throughout the land, it seems that God fulfils his promise to her and, after a year, she gives birth to a son, Isaac (I'm going to go along with the assumption that it's Abraham's son, but with their method of extortion, I have an element of doubt about this). On the eighth day, Abraham circumcised the little bugger as God commanded, and all was happy for a while.

Isaac grew and was weaned, and on that day Abe held a big feast. However, Sarah noticed that the child Abraham whelped to Hagar was "mocking", so she told Abe to get rid of them, *"for that woman's son will never share in the inheritance with my son, Isaac." (Gen. 21:10).* What a nasty thing to do, yet she can blame nobody but herself. SHE was the one who was barren, and offered her slave as a surrogate; SHE was the one whose nose got out of joint when he went there and knocked up the slave girl; SHE was the one whoring out her body to any king that would have her in order to extort money out of them. And now she has a son of her own, she is looking at all her ill-gotten gains and decides that only her blood should inherit it. Can we truly expect anything more from such a nasty piece of work? Abraham's a little pissed about it, because technically the slave's child is his by blood, if not Sarah's. But working under the mindset of, "Happy Wife, Happy Life" (and a brief sob-session with the G man) he sends Hagar and her child off into the Desert of Beersheba with some food and a waterbag, catch'ya bye and thanks for coming (Gen. 21:14).

Okay, let's play a game: let's see if you can spot where the author's choice of phrase ties in with a future event in the following stanzas. Here we go:

When the water in the skin was gone (Gen. 21:15), Hagar put the child down under one of the bushes. She then went off and sat down about a bowshot away, for she thought she cannot watch the boy die, and began to sob (21:16). God heard the kid bawling, and the angel of God (deputy?) called down from heaven (must have a loud voice to cover that distance), told her not to cry, God's heard the kid, go and take his hand, and he'll be made into a great nation (21:18). She opened her eyes, saw some water in front of her, and gave the kid a drink. (21:19). God was with the boy as he grew up. He lived in the desert and became an archer (21:20).

Did you see it? Of course you did, you perceptive readers! The author's unwitting use of the phrase "about a bowshot" – a weapon not mentioned anywhere in the bible until now, although we know from archaeological sites that humans were using them in Africa up to 70,000 years ago – and then, amazingly and completely coincidentally, the child grows up to be an archer. I know it's a small thing, but the devil is in the details. The author could just as easily have used the phrase "a short distance away" or "out of sight" or even "out of earshot" of this child so as not to witness its death from dehydration and exposure, and yet he uses "about a bowshot". There's no reason to use such a phrase other than to conclude that he's making it up as he goes along. He's got the idea that the kid will be an archer which will perhaps play into the story later, and so the phrase was already in the front of his mind, ready for use.

There's also some minor dispute between Abe and Abimelek concerning some wells here. Quite boring actually (pun unintentional), Abimelek asks for some assurances from Abe that he won't screw with him again like last time, and Abe gives him seven female sheep to say that Abe had dug a certain well. The interesting thing is that the place where their oaths were sworn was then called Beersheba, despite it being called that already when Hagar was sent off into it years previously. Timekeeping and simple orderly progression, apparently, remains a problem for the author of the bible. Anyway, treaties were made, oaths were sworn, and Abraham lived with the Philistines for "a good long while". Whoopy do.

## Genesis 22: God watches the latest Saw movie, screws with Abe's mind

*"The toxic behaviours were there before you decided to enter into relationships with them. The signs were there. You may have chosen to look the other way, but the signs were there." – P.A. Speers, Type 1 Sociopath – When Difficult People Are More Than Just Difficult People.*

This bible verse takes place "some time later" in which God, no doubt fancying himself as the character Jigsaw from those scary (read:stupid) movies from 2004 onward, calls on Abraham and tests his faith (Gen. 22:1 – 22:2):

G: Abe!

Abe: Right here, G, wassup?

G: Take your son, your only son whom you love - Isaac - and go to the region of Moriah. Sacrifice him there as a burnt offering on the mountain I will show you.

Abe: [dumbfounded] Dafuq is wrong with you, G, seriously..?!?!

G: Don't question me, bitch, just do it, k…?! (or words to that effect. An insane giggle may have been uttered at some stage.)

And the next morning, he packs up his donkey, grabs Isaac and a couple of servants and heads off to the Mountains of Moriah (shameless Lord of the Rings pun intended). After a few days he spots the mountain and tells the servants to hang back with the donkey while he and Isaac go to the mountain *"to worship and then we will come back to you" (Gen. 22:5)*. Okay, obviously at this stage Abe doesn't expect he will actually sacrifice Isaac, or he would not have said that WE will come back to you. And why would he think otherwise, after all the crap he went through to have a son through Sarah and believing that God had somehow "allowed" Sarah to have this kid? But then God has been seriously mentally unstable for a long time, so who knows what's ticking away in that time bomb of a head of his? Or, he wants to be able to hide the deed from the servants, claiming Isaac fell off a cliff or some shit to save face. Who knows, but somewhere in his mind Abe is running the numbers, and he is not liking the answers he's arriving at.

So Abe and Isaac are heading up to this mountain, and Isaac notices the wood and the fire for the burnt offering, but no sacrificial lamb, and brings it to his father's attention. To which Abe replied, *"God himself will provide the lamb for the burnt offering, my son." (Gen. 22:8)*. Shrugging his shoulders (probably), Isaac followed his father to wherever it was they were going. When they finally reached the place God told Abraham about, he created the altar and set the wood upon it; then bound his son Isaac and placed him on top.

As Abraham was reaching for the knife to kill his son, God called out to Abraham and yelled, "PSYCH!!!!!" No, not really, but if this was all happening today, he probably would have. No, he merely said, *"Do not lay a hand on the boy. Do not do anything to him. Now I know that you fear God, because you have not withheld from me your son, your only son." (Gen. 22:12)*. Abraham looked up and noticed at that time a ram caught in a nearby thicket, so he sacrificed that instead and summarily called the place, "The Lord Will Provide". Then there was more of the "your descendants will be more numerous than the stars in the sky" spiel and "you'll own the cities of your enemies" crap and blessed-is-thee blah blah blah, and they went back and stayed a while in Beersheba (because who wouldn't want to stay in a place with Beer in it?)

Surely, of all the passages in the bible, this one most accurately describes the mindlessness of modern-day religious fanatics, that they will slaughter their own families if they get it in their head that God told them to do it. Such complete, unquestioning obsequiousness is dangerous in the wrong hands; for example, the hands of an invisible man in the sky. It is little wonder that clergymen the world over refer to their parishioners as their "flock", for they are surely being led to the slaughter, just like any other unquestioning sheep.

Do you think I am exaggerating, dear reader? There was a case some years ago when a deeply-religious teenager walked into the bathroom without realizing his mother was in the bath, and saw her naked. His solution: to cauterize both his eyes with a red-hot screwdriver. If one were to troll through case studies of these sorts of things, you'll find that a startling percentage of self-mutilations are related to religious teachings. Additionally, auto-enucleations in particular have a very close association with schizophrenic disorders. And to be perfectly honest, you'd need to be encumbered with some major mental short-circuits to gouge your own eyes out or sacrifice your own child or, god forbid, take a knife to your own wedding tackle. Yes, I'm looking at you, Abe, you sick bastard; now take your haloperidol or we'll put you in the padded tent again.

Some time after these questionable events, Abraham was informed that his brother Nahor had fathered sons to his wife Milkah who, if you will recall, was also his niece, she being the daughter of Nahor's brother Haran. There were eight sons all up, called Uz, Buz (perhaps original proprietors of the purple-coloured drive-thru coffee shops?) Kemuel, Kesed, Hazo, Pildashbut, Jidlaph and Bethuel. The important one was Bethuel, who in turn spawned a daughter called Rebekah whom we shall discuss later. He had some kids from a concubine as well, but I'll refrain from mentioning them in any detail, until they become relevant to the plot of course.

## Genesis 23: The Death of Sarah

*"I do not fear death. I had been dead for billions and billions of years before I was born, and had not suffered the slightest inconvenience from it."* –Mark Twain.

We're told in this chapter of the death of Sarah, Abe's old squeeze and partner in extortion, at the ripe old age of one hundred and twenty seven. Thing is, she apparently died in Hebron in the land of Canaan, and Abe went to mourn and weep over her.

My question right off the bat is, when did Abe and Sarah go their separate ways? Why was Abe so far away from his wife? The last we heard, he was kicking back in Gerar near Beershaba after booting his sex slave into the desert with his slave son Ishmael, then shipping off to live with the Philistines, committing impromptu filicide and having a grand old time of it. When along this journey did Abe just leave Sarah by the side of the road? Aren't they supposed to be a team act, extorting any kings in their path, using God as their hired goon? No matter, the partnership is ended, and Abe treats with the Hittites for a spot to bury his dead. Although the Hittites are happy to let him bury his woman anywhere in Canaan, he ends up paying 400 shekels to some dude called Ephron for a cave in a field so he can bury her there. Certainly he's losing his touch if he's now having to pay for stuff, but I suppose he'll have to get used to that now, at least until he can find another partner in crime. I wonder if Abe was tempted to hook up with Hagar again now that his main squeeze was out of the picture? Any normal human would, but then we've already established that Abe isn't exactly playing with a full deck, as it were.

## Genesis 24: Isaac and Rebekah, sitting in a tree: incest runs in the family.

*"Incest is rape by extortion. Thus the child's very childhood becomes a weapon used to control her." – E. Sue Blume, Secret Survivors.*

We return to Crazy Old Abe, who is very old now. He *"said to his most senior servant, the one who was in charge of all that he had, 'Put your hand under my thigh.'"* (Gen. 24:2). He went on to make the servant swear by the Lord that he would not get a wife for his son Isaac from the daughters of the Canaanites (they really *did* have it in for poor old Canaan, didn't they?) but to find a woman from Abraham's own country. He wasn't to take Isaac there, of course - that would be too easy - but the servant would have to go and just find an unmarried woman and drag her back for Isaac. Crazy old Abe..

Okay, now if you're like me, you were probably wondering at first why Abraham wanted the servant to put his hand under Abe's thigh. Sounds like a silly thing to do, really, until we remember Abraham's covenant with God. We're not referring to thighs here, dear readers, but loins or, more specifically, testicles. Abraham's (and hence, Hebrew) oaths apparently required the servant to swear on the covenantal circumcision; to swear upon seed of the master, and therefore had to put their hands on Abe's meat-and-two-veg as a binding oath of compliance. And how clever of Abraham to use his self-mutilation as a mystical covenant to gratify his sexual urges, whereas other creepy old men not blessed by God (or schizophrenia) had no options other than to scream, "Grab my nuts!!" at passers-by and hope for the best.

Expunging these images of grabbing elderly genitalia from our minds (preferably, with a soldering iron or a cheese grater), we return to the servant, who after swearing oath in this most unpleasant manner loaded up some camels and headed off to the town of Nahor (named, obviously, after Nahor) to find a suitable wife for Isaac. Not having the faintest idea of how he was supposed to find this perfect woman for his master's son, he prays to God in an effort to find the right one; he kneels the camels down at a well outside the city, and implores God to make the right woman say the right thing. In this case, he implores God to make her freely offer to water his camels in addition to his asking for a drink just for himself. Amazingly, this tactic works, and the Chosen One turns out to be an unmarried woman called….. Rebekah. Yes, *that* Rebekah, daughter of Bethuel, son of Milkah, who is niece-wife to Nahor, brother of Abraham. Either through sheer accident or malevolent intent from on-high, the chosen wife for Isaac is actually his first cousin once- AND twice-removed, or to put it simply, Isaac's father's great grandniece. In the simplest terms possible, it would be as if you went over to your cousin's place and married her granddaughter, because technically-speaking Milkah is Isaac's cousin; yet she is also married to his uncle, so it really depends on where you want to put her on the generational tree. These things confuse me at the best of times, especially when you start with all this once- and twice-removed business. And when you bring in-breeding to the mix, it gets ugly real fast, cleft-palates and mental disorders (in particular, schizophrenia) notwithstanding.

Now if the "senior servant" in Abraham's household was any kind of servant at all, he should have known the familial relationships of the house he serves: who is a daughter, who is a son, who is a niece, who is a cousin, whatever. It's not so populated a world at this stage that he wouldn't know the immediate family, or at least heard of them through Abe's tales and/or ranting. If this woman has identified herself as Rebekah daughter of Milkah, wouldn't a savvy servant instantly realise that he's talking to his master Isaac's cousin, and too closely related to be considered marriage material (although that didn't stop Nahor, did it?) This servant nevertheless talks his way back to the Nahor household (tenthold?) and after a long and complicated retelling of the tale and much bartering, the servant was able to secure Rebekah for his master's son's wife. And another time-paradox for you, in Genesis 24:67: *"Isaac brought her into the tent of his mother Sarah, and he married Rebekah. So she became his wife and he loved her; and Isaac was comforted after his mother's death."* The passage indicates that Isaac brought Rebekah into his mother's tent, i.e. to meet his mother Sarah. But we know from the previous Genesis chapter that Sarah is dead and buried in a cave by this time, and I can't imagine Abe leaving a tent standing about unused, and honestly, why go to a tent in the first place other than to meet its occupant? I'm guessing Isaac surely had his own tent by now, so it would have been more logical just to take her to his tent and do his thing, would it not? So we either have an unused shrine of a tent to honour his dead wife and to creep out other relatives, or we have a time paradox, assuming the bible is attempting to follow the course of events as they allegedly happened. In the course of normal conversation with another person, we will naturally, from time to time, forget an important event when recounting our adventures, and we will often digress from our topic with remarks like, "Oh yeah wait, before that, x happened…" or similar asides. With the written word, we have the luxury of inserting the missing digressions as we remember them, and thus can more accurately tell our tales. So why the disparities in the timeline? Or perhaps the author simply forgot that Sarah was dead and buried by this time. Who knows..?

Incidentally, this is the first instance where a woman has covered herself with a veil (Gen. 24:65). No previous passage has mentioned the wearing of any kind of veil or the reason she would wear it, or what Rebekah was doing exposed to the lusts of random males if veils were required in mixed company. Certainly there was never a requirement for Sarah to be veiled anywhere she went; indeed, she used her unveiledness to great financial (if unethical) effect in duping multiple kings out of their livestock and slaves. So why now? There seems to be a lot of extra rules and conditions being made up behind the scenes of which we are unaware. Hopefully further passages will shed some light on this.

## Genesis 25: Crazy Old Abe Kicks the Bucket

*"I get very annoyed when people think I'm nice or diffident or a polite English gentleman. I'm a nasty piece of work, and people should know that."* –Hugh Grant.

At some stage between the death of Sarah and the death of himself, Abraham managed to score another wife, Keturah, and fathered six more children. Abe himself ended up living one hundred and seventy five years, gave gifts to his concubines' whelps, left everything else to Isaac, and summarily died; after which his sons Isaac and Ishmael (the one sent away to die, of which no mention has been made until this event) buried him in the cave next to Sarah. Isaac then scored the blessing of God after Abe's demise, Isaac being parked up near Beer Lahai Roi.

Of Ishmael, there's not much to tell. He had his own brood (whom I won't bother to identify unless they're suddenly relevant to the plot), lived one hundred and thirty seven years and then died. He was buried somewhere east of Egypt, and his tribe lived in hostility toward all tribes related to them. Probably they're still pissed off about their patriarch being sent into the desert to die. Old hatreds die hard, after all, and bitterness can set in against those not of your kind, so that eventually your great-great-

great-great-great grandkids end up losing their legs and hunting white whales. Perhaps.

## Jacob and Esau: Birthright is thicker than Blood

It seems that meanness runs deep in some families. Whether it's some malicious trait that is inherited through one's DNA or something that's learned from our environment and family as we grow, is up to debate. What is absolutely certain, however, is that this nastiness has been undeniably passed on down Abraham's line.

Isaac was forty when he married Rebekah, and after twenty years of praying because she was childless (another side-effect of such inbreeding is reduced fertility rate and increased incidence of spontaneous abortion), she ended up having twins, Esau and Jacob. Esau, the first one out, grew to become a strong hairy hunter while his brother Jacob preferred to stay among the tents of home. As Isaac had a penchant for wild game, he was fonder of Esau, whilst Rebekah was fond of Jacob, probably for the simple fact that he was around more for her to bond with him.

One day, while Jacob was kicking back cooking some stew, his brother Esau came back from a hunt and implored to his brother, *"Quick, let me have some of that red stew! I'm famished!" (Gen. 25:30)*. Jacob, however, replied, "First, sell me your birthright."

"Look, I am about to die. What good is the birthright to me?"

"Swear to me first."

So Esau traded his birthright for a mess of pottage (some lentil stew and a hunk of bread), and this is why nerds will always prevail over jocks in the end. And while I can appreciate that brothers are often competitive by nature, it does seem a tad excessive to demand a birthright for a simple bowl of lentils. Esau being the older (and stronger) brother, you would think that he could have just bludgeoned his way to the lentil pot and helped himself, if he was that hungry. The hunters of that era weren't known for their refined social graces, after all; just slap your little shit of a brother upside the head, seat yourself proprietorially at the pot, and eat the damn lentils. But no, he brashly gives away his inheritance for a bowl of stew. Besides the lack of social graces, it would seem intelligence isn't high on the prerequisites to become a hunter.

## Genesis 26: Isaac and Abimelek: Like father, like son

*"Insanity is Hereditary. You get it from your kids."*
–Sam Levenson.

This bible passage is essentially a carbon-copy of Geneses 12 and 20: it's only the players have changed. There was another famine in the land, and God appears to Isaac and tells him not to go into Egypt, but to *"live in the land where I tell you to live" (Gen. 26:2)*, does his usual numerous descendants bullshit blessing again, so as a result Isaac stayed in Gerar. Then in a bad case of Deja-vu, the men of Gerar ask about Isaac's wife and he tells then, "She is my sister." Well, we know how this old chestnut is going to turn out, don't we, readers? Abimelek later finds Isaac caressing Rebekah, drags him in and asks why Isaac lied about her, gets told (AGAIN) that he was afraid for his life; and Abimelek gave him lots of land and goods (AGAIN), and Isaac became extremely rich (AGAIN) through lies and deception no doubt learned through his father Abraham.

I mean seriously, is this Abimelek guy a slow learner or what? After all, those who do not learn from their mistakes are doomed to repeat them, and this is the second time he's been duped like this. He can't be much of a leader if he keeps falling for the same old shtick time and time again. And just how old is this guy, anyway? Abimelek was a king long before even Abe came onto the scene with his fraud act; Abe died when he was 175 (despite God imposing an age limit on humans of a mere 120 years, back in Gen. 6:3) and was around 80 or 90 when he duped Abimelek the first time. It's time this guy stepped up to the king plate and tells this fraudster that if he tries that shit again, the pain of his circumcision will be an orgasm compared to what molestations he'll visit on his person. But that's just what I would do in his place; sadly, I'm a king only between my ears.

The Philistines, in the meantime, have seen Isaac's ill-gotten rise to wealth and power, and retaliate by filling in all the wells Abraham's servants dug when he was there last. Abimelek, for his part, finally grows some stones and tells Isaac to shove off, because *"you have become too powerful for us" (Gen. 26:16)*. Well, not stones, perhaps - he was just scared that Isaac would use his wealth and power to usurp his kingship (don't you just love the human instinct of self-preservation?). So Isaac bundled up all his bits and settled in the valley nearby and reopened the wells that were filled in. He dug some other wells too and discovered water, but the local herders argued and claimed the water as their own; this happened a couple more times before he dug one nobody disputed. He named it Rehoboth (god knows why), and then headed to Beersheba.

God pokes his nose in again with more of his blessing crap, and it transpired that Abimelek had come over for a visit with his senior advisor. Isaac asked what he was doing there considering he was told to shove off, and Abi said that he saw that "god was with Isaac" and decided that there ought to be a sworn agreement between them – a non-aggression pact, if you will. So they ate and drank on this deal, the servants dug another well which found water, they called it Shibah, and *"and to this day the name of the name of the town has been Beersheba"* (Gen. 26:33). *sigh* Again, Beersheba was called that long before any of this happened, but who am I to argue the renaming of the same spot with the same name over and over again for eternity? We finish off this passage with Esau marrying someone called Judith, and another called Basemath (first instance of polygamy?) when he was forty. It is said that they were a source of grief to Isaac and Rebekah, but to be honest, I consider it to be well-deserved karma coming home to roost.

## Genesis 27: Jacob screws Esau yet again

*"Evil is a miscellaneous collection of nasty things that nasty people do." –Richard Dawkins.*

We join this passage with Isaac as an old, blind man on his deathbed. He summons his favourite son Esau and tells him of his impending death. He implores the boy to head out with his bow and kill and prepare "the tasty food he likes to eat" and bring it to him, so that he may give Esau his blessing before he dies.

Unfortunately for Isaac, his wife Rebekah overhears this, and when Esau heads off, she summons *her* favourite son Jacob and tells him what has transpired. She tells him to get some choice goats from the flock and bring them to her so that she can prepare this so-called "tasty meal", and Jacob can give it to his father in order to receive Esau's blessing. When Jacob points out that Esau is in fact a hairy lout whereas Jacob is smooth of skin, Rebekah tells him to wear some goatskin over his arms to trick the blind old fool into thinking that Jacob is really Esau. So all these things are prepared, and Jacob faces his father in the tent.

The old bugger might be blind but he's not stupid. He can hear that it's Jacob's voice, and questions how he killed the game so quickly, but with simple assurances (the Lord gave me success) he gets past that. He is asked to come close so he can touch him, and Isaac feels the goat hair and is fooled once again. Then he asks Jacob to kiss his father, and the smell of the goatskin fools him a third time. Isaac summarily gives Jacob the blessing intended for Esau.

And just in time, it would seem. Jacob had "scarcely left his father's presence" when Esau came back from his goat hunting, tasty meal in hand. When he implored his father to partake of the meal, Isaac was all like, "Who are you?"

"It's your son, Esau."

"Who was it then that hunted game and brought it to me? I ate it just before you came and I blessed him – and indeed he will be blessed!"

Esau then figured out what had happened, and implored his father to bless him too, but to no avail. Isaac said, "Your brother came deceitfully and took your blessing." Now Esau was royally PISSED. Having first taken his birthright, and now his blessing, he asked, "Have you reserved no blessing for me?" To which Isaac replied that he had, "made Jacob lord over you and have made all his relatives his servants, so what can I possibly do for you, my son?" Esau then made his own oath that, when Isaac was dead and properly mourned, he would kill his brother Jacob. Naturally, Rebekah got wind of this and implored Jacob to *"flee at once to my brother Laban in Harran" (Gen. 28:43)* until Esau cooled down (yeah, fat chance of that). Rebekah then gives Isaac a serve, saying she's "disgusted with living because of these Hittite women".

Really?! Does NOBODY in this book take any responsibility for their own deplorable actions? I ask again, what are we trying to teaching our children when we thrust this tripe down their young throats? That it's okay to screw people over if you can get away with it? To dishonour your own siblings and to blatantly steal what is theirs by right? That it's okay to commit fraud, to lie, and then put the blame on others when they get caught out? To commit incestuous acts with impunity? If these are the kinds of lessons contained in this book, I'm glad I was never exposed to it when I was of an impressionable age, and it reflects badly on those who DID grow up with these lessons crammed into them.

## Genesis 28: Esau spite-marries, Jacob dreams and inbreeds

*"Instead of a man of peace and love, I have become a man of violence and revenge." –Hiawatha.*

We start this chapter with Isaac summoning Jacob to his side, and getting the usual blessing and then being commanded: *"Do not marry a Canaanite woman. Go at once to Paddan Aram to the house of your mother's father Bethuel. Take yourself a wife there, from the daughters of Laban, your mother's brother." (Gen. 28:2)*. Oh look, *another* anomaly; how unexpected! Were we not just told that it was Rebekah who told Jacob to "flee at once" to her brother in Gen. 28:43? If this is the case, how could Isaac possibly have then told Jacob the same thing, especially if he was in haste to escape Esau's murderous intent? Furthermore, he tells Jacob not only to do this, but to find a wife among the daughters of his uncle - to again breed with a first-cousin, worsening the already rampant homozygosity endemic in the Abraham ancestry. One can only imagine the deformed monstrosities being spawned by these people; but if you don't have much of an imagination, try typing, "images inbreeding in humans" into a Google search if you get a moment, and prepare to be disturbed.

Again, I am inclined to ask what sort of moral message this book is sending to our children? I mean sure, you could maintain that we're all descended in one way or another from the occupants of the ark (assuming, for the moment, the ark thing actually happened) but there are certainly a lot of people floating about the place that don't seem to be related to Abe's line at all. If everyone else was supposed to have drowned in the flood, where did they all come from? Simple breeding can't adequately explain the population numbers, especially when these people don't seem to recall where they came from ancestrally speaking.

But I digress; even as Jacob is being told (either by Rebekah or Isaac, depending on which passage you prefer) to go and make some more deformed babies, Esau gets wind of all this, and learns of his father's distaste for Canaanite women. So like any good, spiteful, disinherited son, he heads off to Isaac's half-brother Ishmael and ends up marrying Ishmael's daughter Mahalath, *"in addition to the wives he already had" (Gen. 28:9)*. Okay, so this is technically marrying his HALF-cousin, but as Crazy Old Abe's blood is in both of them, it's still incest; it's like your first son's son going to your second son and marrying that son's daughter. Sick and twisted. This is the kind of shit you're telling your kids is acceptable behaviour, every time you put a bible in front of them as a guide to moral living. Seriously, you're better off letting them play in traffic than being anywhere near a bible.

## Jacob's Led Zeppelin dream

On his way to Harran, Jacob had occasion to stop for the night at a place previously, apparently, called Luz. Grabbing a nearby stone for a pillow, he went to sleep and dreamed of the proverbial stairway to heaven, with the usual angels going up and down on it. At the top of these stairs (naturally) was God, who called Jacob and blessed him again and started handing out real estate again; this time the land Jacob was lying on, as well as all the tiresome promises of descendants more numerous than the dust and blah blah blah blah blah. Jacob woke from this dream and was afraid, saying *"How awesome is this place! This is none other than the house of God; this is the gate to heaven" (Gen. 28:17)*. So in the morning he made an altar out of his stone-pillow, poured oil on it and called the place Bethel. Additionally, he promised that of all that would come to him, he would give God a tenth (Gen. 28:22).

Interesting to note here that, for the deeply indoctrinated members of Christianity (especially born-again Christians), this must be the go-to verse their church refers to when they collect (read: extort) one tenth of their parishioner's wages, paid automatically into parish funds. And these people are perfectly happy to just give away their hard-earned money, as if buying their way into heaven is a valid thing, like purchasing a ticket on a celestial airline. Good luck with that, guys, but if you've been a prick to people all your life and you think you can just buy your way into paradise expecting to be welcomed and accepted by those who got there by being nice, think again (assuming the whole heaven/hell dichotomy actually exists, of course).

## Genesis 29: Jacob reaches Paddan Aram, gets two-for-one offer

*"Bigamy is having one spouse too many. Monogamy is the same."* –Oscar Wilde.

Our intrepid blessing-usurper Jacob finally reaches Paddan Aram after his brief faffing about in the desert near Luz. After a brief and uninteresting conversation with some shepherds in relation to a stone-blocked well, he finds Rachel, daughter of Laban and explains his intentions. He is summarily brought into the household and introduced to his uncle Laban, and the whole boring tale is repeated.

Jacob was welcomed as family (as he undoubtedly was) and stayed about a month, after which Laban considered it bad form to expect Jacob to work for him for nothing, so he asked Jacob what his wages should be. Jacob replied, *"I'll work for you for seven years in return for your daughter Rachel" (Gen. 29:18).* Laban agreed to this; and after seven years of toil, he held a great feast for the consummation of this incestuous union. Laban, however had other ideas, and when Jacob went to bed, he sent his older daughter, Leah, into his bed.

Of course, Jacob consummated the hell out of who he thought was Rachel. But in the morning he discovered it was the older daughter he'd done the dirty, filthy Dirty with (he must have been blind-drunk to confuse the sisters in such close conditions, but meh). When he confronted Laban on this deception, Laban replied that *"it is not our custom to give the younger daughter in marriage before the older one. Finish this daughter's bridal week; then we'll give you the younger daughter too, in exchange for another seven years of work."* (Gen. 28:26 – 28:27). Because Jacob wanted Rachel all along and figured, 'in for a penny, in for a pound,' he laboured another seven years for Laban and scored the other daughter into the deal.

Now God pokes his beak into the affairs of men yet again. Because he sees that Leah is the unloved wife, he "enabled" her to conceive while keeping Rachel childless. This kid she named Reuben, because apparently the lord saw Leah's misery, and that surely Jacob will love her now (the traditional Hebrew meaning is, "Behold, a son": how this relates to the mother's misery is unknown). Leah repeats this mantra three more times, birthing Simeon, Levi and Judah, although whether subsequent sons made Jacob love Leah more, only Jacob would know.

## Genesis 30: Sibling rivalry kicks up a notch or eight

*"The jealous are troublesome to others, but a torment to themselves."* –William Penn.

In this chapter, Rachel is seeing her older sister popping out kids to Jacob and the old green-eyed monster, Jealousy, rears its ugly head. She fronts Jacob and tells him, *"Give me children, or I'll die!" (Gen. 30:2)*. Jacob gets angry with her and says, "Am I in the place of God, who has kept you from having children?" So Rachel, in a very Sarai-esque manoeuvre, offers up her servant Bilbah as a surrogate, to have children vicariously through her. Jacob falls for it just as Abe did with Hagar and got the servant with a son, Dan. Luckily Jacob dodges a bullet because Rachel feels vindicated with the birth, and there are no hard feelings with the servant. When a second kid was birthed, Rachel feels she has had "a great struggle" with her sister, and had won (Gen. 30:8).

Leah, by this stage, has seen what Rachel's game is and in retaliation she offers her own servant, Zilpah, to the same effect, and thus two more kids are spawned. An odd way to vindicate and revenge yourself upon your own sibling, but then who really knows how they thought back then? Nowadays siblings tend to limit themselves to ripping each other's hair out or pouring bleach on their sibling's pot plant, or hiding spiders under their pillows (well, rocks if Jacob's pillow is any indication). Who am I to judge, but to my mind there better ways to revenge yourself than Childbirth at Ten Paces.

Now at one stage of the wheat harvest, Reuben finds some mandrake plants and brings them home to his mother Leah. Rachel spots these plants and asks for them, but Leah is refuses, feeling that Rachel has *"stolen her husband away"* – stupid I know, because BOTH of them are his wives (and first-cousins). Anyway, Rachel offers up Jacob for a night in the sack in exchange for these mandrake plants, the deal is made, and before you can say how's-your-father, Leah pops out three more kids (Gen. 30:14 – 30:21).

A quick note at this point about mandrake plants, if I may. All species of mandrake, or *mandragora*, are highly active tropane alkaloids, which gives them anticholinergic, hallucinogenic and hypnotic properties, making them poisonous to humans, predominantly the roots and leaves of the plant. A particularly bad anticholinergic reaction can lead to asphyxia, while the more common effects of ingestion are headache, vomiting, diarrhoea, tachycardia, hyperactivity and hallucinations. Why Rachel would want this plant is a mystery unless she intends conducting some clandestine poisoning and/or witchcraft rituals in the near future.

A more likely explanation here is that Rachel has mistaken the plant for the similar-looking ginseng plant, which is reputed to have fertility enhancing properties and better explains why she was willing to offer Leah a tumble in the sack with Jacob in exchange for a few plants. It seems they weren't overly effective as a fertility catalyst, because it was some years before God "remembered" Rachel and allowed her to conceive her own son, whom she named Joseph.

**Part 2: What the flock..?!**

This part of Genesis 30 is wildly confusing to say the least, and if you have the ability to access a bible without it (or you) bursting into flames, I would invite you to explore this verse and see if you can make any better sense of it than me. It is difficult in the extreme to determine accurately what Laban did and what Jacob did in relation to the splitting of the flock and the actions taken thereafter, and what flocks went with whom, so I'll try to decipher it as best I can. Here goes…

It starts with Jacob approaching his uncle Laban and begging permission to leave with his cousin-wives and children and head off back to his own household that he has neglected for the last fourteen years. Laban demurs, as Jacob has done a bucket-load of work for him and has made him wealthy in his own right. Jacob points this out, of course; so after a protracted bout haggling and haranguing, Jacob suggests that his wages should be all the spotted and streaked animals from Laban's flocks, leaving the pure white ones for Laban. Laban readily agrees to this, and so the next day Laban splits the flock and places the speckled and streaked ones in the care of his sons. Then Laban put a three day journey between himself and Jacob for reasons unknown, whilst Jacob tended the rest of Laban's pure flocks (Gen. 30:25 – 30:36).

As far as I can make out, from how it is set out in the bible I'm referencing:

* Laban agrees to give Jacob all the spotted animals as wages;

* Laban separates the spotted animals and puts them in the care of his own sons;

* Laban heads three days' journey away from Jacob, who is looking after Laban's (pure) flock.

The immediate question is why Jacob didn't just take receipt of his wages (the striped flocks) and head back home, his work complete? Another is why Laban has retained ownership of the striped flocks through his sons, and why Jacob is continuing to tend Laban's flocks if his labours are complete? This doesn't make any sense if the contract of employment has been completed. If you have a better interpretation, I am all ears; however, the reason for Jacob's continuing tending of Laban's "pure" flocks becomes evident in the rest of the chapter.

Whilst tending these pure flocks alone, Jacob grabbed some poplar, almond and plane tree branches and peeled the bark on them to expose the white inner wood of the branches. He then put these striped branches at all the waterholes so that, when the pure animals came to drink and if they were in season, the animals would mate in front of these striped branches and through some mystical optical imprinting, the offspring would be as striped and speckled as the branches (the bible's first known record of Material Impression, and the precursor to Genetic Theory). Jacob then further refined this research by only putting his branches out when the strongest of Laban's animals were in heat, and removing them when the weakest rocked up for a drink. We are led to believe that this method of selective breeding through visual stimulus resulted in Jacob acquiring large, strong flocks of sheep, goats, servants, camels and whatever else Jacob could persuade to breed in front of a bunch of striped sticks in the ground.

If I have the passages interpreted correctly, then it's all a little silly, isn't it? Today, of course, we know about genetic reproduction, dominant and recessive genes, DNA and RNA, and can easily explain how two pure white sheep can spawn a speckled one, or how two parents with dominant brown eyes can spawn a blue-eyed child by passing on their respective recessive blue-eyed genetic sequences, for example:

If B = Brown RNA (dominant gene)

And b – blue RNA (recessive gene)

And if Parent A: Bb -> brown eyes

And if Parent B: Bb -> brown eyes

Child combinations -> BB (brown eyes), Bb or bB (brown eyes), and bb (blue eyes).

This is somewhat simplistic, but is sufficient to illustrate how genetic inheritance works. It also explains why Jacob would think he had some measure of success with his clandestine Striped Stick Technique designed to screw Laban out of his good breeding stock, when the real cause was occurring at the cellular level and far beyond his ability to manipulate. That is, unless Jacob had tagged and numbered every single animal and made incredibly detailed records of the husbandry of those animals in the fourteen years of his stay with his uncle, although there is no mention of this in the bible; and if there were written records they would surely have perished long ago unless they were hidden alongside the Dead Sea Scrolls or something. Whichever way you interpret these happenings, it is nevertheless another magnificent example of moral integrity for our children:

Even if you get a pretty good deal for your work, keep trying to screw them over for more, and family loyalty be damned.

## Genesis 31: The gig is up

*"Doesn't the fight for survival also justify swindle and theft? In self defence, anything goes." –Imelda Marcos.*

It isn't long before Jacob overhears Laban's sons complaining that he has *"taken everything our father owned and taken all this wealth from what belonged to our father" (Gen. 31:1)*. Jacob himself, apparently, also noticed that Laban's attitude towards him was not what it had been. What seals the deal for Jacob is a convenient visit from God, who tells him to high-tail it back to Canaan with all his ill-gotten goodies.

Jacob sends for this cousin-wives who meet him in the fields, and he bitches about how hard he's worked and how Laban has changed the deal of his wages "ten times". He then claims that God has *"taken away your father's livestock and given them to me" (Gen. 31:9)*. Highly amusing stuff, considering Jacob has been using his fundamentally-flawed Striped Stick Method to steal any remaining flocks belonging to Laban. He says they have to gather up their (ill-gotten) flocks and vamoose back to Jacob's father in Canaan. Rachel and Leah question whether they still have entitlement to their father's inheritance, thinking that they are now foreigners; and so when they're ready to run, and Laban heads off to shear his sheep, *"Rachel stole her father's household gods" (Gen. 31:19)*.

That's "gods", not "goods". Gods. Plural. At first glance, the average person might mistake this for a typo, because there is only supposed to be one god, and from what we've read so far it would be highly unlikely that he'd be kicking around Laban's house somewhere. He's got things to do and people to smite and so on. Further exploration of this reveals that "gods" might refer to Laban's teraphim, which are essentially items or symbols of special religious significance. The theory here is that Rachel stole these teraphim so as to enable them to sneak off without her father using them to divine the direction of their flight, especially as Jacob took pains not to tell Laban that he was slinking off like a thief in the night. It's an interesting thing because this is the first instance of humans using objects as divining tools and oracles, essentially the precursor to crystal balls, scrying stones and all manner of things normally associated with witchcraft. Although to be honest, if Laban has more than two brain cells to rub together, he would deduce by pure logic that Jacob was pissing off back to his old man with all his ill-gotten gains; and even if he wasn't, Isaac would be the first point-of-call anyway to either assist in finding Jacob or to seek reparations if the search failed. As it turns out, Jacob by this stage had taken all his ill-gotten goodies across the Euphrates River and towards Gilead.

## Laban catches on, the chase ensues

It took three days for Laban to discover Jacob's hasty exodus. Fortunately for Laban, he did have more than two brain cells to rub together and took off with his relatives and eventually caught up with Jacob in Gilead. Just prior to Jacob's apprehension, however, God sticks his beak in again and warns Laban *"not to say anything to Jacob, either good or bad" (Gen. 31:24).* Really? He's going to just catch up with him over tea and scones and discuss the weather? Like HELL, he's going with the intention of ripping Jacob a very large new one. But Laban manages to get a grip (if only on the threat of being turned into salt or something) and apprehends the absconding Jacob.

Laban's pretty diplomatic for the most part, and asks Jacob why he snuck off when he could have been sent off with love and harps and shit, and also asks why Jacob stole his gods (his teraphim, scrying devices, oracles, witchcraft tools, whatever). Jacob answers that he was afraid Laban wouldn't let him keep his cousin-wives, but adds a caveat that anyone who stole Laban's gods will be put to death, and gives Laban the run of the camp to find his lost shit.

At this stage of the game, Jacob didn't know that Rachel had filched her dad's soothsaying trinkets, that she had hidden them under the saddle of the poor camel she was sitting on.

When her father came out of her tent, Rachel used the Woman's Excuse (possibly for the first time in recorded history): *"Don't be angry, my lord, that I cannot stand up in your presence; I'm having my period." (Gen. 31:35)*. So, not only has she married her cousin who was already married to her own sister, she stole from her father AND lied to his face about it when confronted with discovery. What a wonderful role model she is for our children! Anyway, Jacob loses his shit now and berates Laban for keeping him tied up for twenty years working for his kids and his flocks, forever changing his wages, and a myriad other slights both real and imagined. Laban for his part claimed that all the stuff Jacob has is his, but sets up a covenant with Jacob. Together they gather up some rocks into a pile and swear that neither will cross the pile to harm the other. Having secured this pact, Laban sods off back to his own place. Well, that was anticlimactic...

## Genesis 32: Jacob tries to buy his life, rolls on the ground with another man

*"Being slightly paranoid is like being slightly pregnant. It tends to get worse."* –Molly Ivins.

So Jacob's heading back to his father's joint, and he meets some angels along the way (will this infernally-meddling god EVER leave us to our own devices?) and uses these angels to send message to his brother Esau of his impending arrival back to his native soil. The angels, of course, acquiesce to Jacob's request and, on their return, inform him that Esau is coming to meet Jacob, along with about four hundred of his mates.

Jacob, of course, shits himself, and summarily divides his camp into two, rationalizing that Esau can only attack one of them, giving the other group time to escape. Then he prays like a condemned man before selecting the choicest animals from his flocks and sending them on ahead of him as a peace offering-cum-shield against his brother's vengeance. Having done that he resumed his praying.

### God feels like a playful tumble

Later that night, Jacob gathers up his cousin-wives, kids and possessions and sent them across the river (it says he *led* them across the Jabbok River, but then it goes on to state that he then sent his possessions across and was left alone on the other side of the river from all his things). Never mind, it's just another example of the author not getting his story straight, so we'll ignore it.

So *"Jacob was left alone, and a man wrestled with him 'til daybreak" (Gen. 32:24)*. Um..... he wasn't alone, was he, if he was rolling around on the ground with some stranger. Also, where did this strange man come from? And if it was truly God as the passage claims him to be, then you have to question his motives and/or mentality. What was God's major malfunction that he thought this was a good idea? How did it even get started? Was there a meeting and general consensus to wrestle, or did God just jump Jacob from behind and they got busy with it? Was there no one else available for him to try out his wrestling skills back at the office? Was God watching some WWE (or the immortal equivalent) and thought it'd be fun to try? Did God create chairs for them to smash over their respective heads? The questions are as endless as they are amusing.

So it turns out that God couldn't beat Jacob at wrestling, despite there being no record anywhere to suggest that this was one of Jacob's regular hobbies, and despite being, well, an omnipotent GOD; and so he cheats and uses the old "touch the hip socket somehow so that it becomes wrenched" manoeuvre, and cries off from the impromptu contest, saying to Jacob in a begging voice, "Let me go, for it is daybreak."

Jacob replies, "I will not let you go unless you bless me."

God then asks Jacob, "What is your name?" (Author's note: REALLY..??!)

Jacob replies, "Jacob."

Then "the man" replies, *"Your name will no longer be Jacob, but Israel, because you have struggled with God and with humans and have overcome"* (Gen. 32:26 – 32:28).

Seriously, God has to stop screwing about with people like this. It's disturbing, it's unnecessary and it's utterly confusing for all concerned. I don't know what God's problem is, but I'll bet it's hard to pronounce. So now, as a result of his nocturnal activities, Jacob is now bizarrely called Israel, he's got a cracking limp because of God's Tendon Touch, and now Israelites won't eat the tendon attached to the socket of the hip because of it. Not that you'd get a lot of nutrition from a hip socket tendon, or even be able to digest it effectively; those suckers are tough and stringy and rubbery unless you boil the crap out of them, after which they turn into a gelatinous goo that is good for nothing but clogging your arteries.

## Genesis 33: Jacob meets Esau, and things get awkward

*"Cunning… is but the low mimic of wisdom." – Plato.*

Jacob (or is it Israel? The bible interchanges these names frequently in this passage) looks up and sees his brother Esau heading towards him with this four hundred mates. So he puts the female servants and children up front, Leah and her kids behind those, and Rachel and her kids behind them. My first thought here was, "human shields" until he then grows a pair and leads the charge, *"bowing down to the ground seven times as he approached his brother" (Gen. 33:3)*. I don't know why he would bow seven times. Perhaps it's a lucky number; perhaps that's all the time he had before Esau reached him; perhaps it's symbolic with some mystical meaning, like, "I'm a thieving shit of a brother who's about to get his deserved comeuppance". Whatever the reason for this, I don't know, nor do I care. But instead of a sword through the heart, Esau embraces his brother and weeps like a child. Who knew?

After the family introductions are made, Esau enquires of the reason for all the flocks, and Jacob says they're gifts to find his brother's favour. Esau's all like, noooo, it's cool, I have my own flocks, and Jacob's like, noooo, I insist, so Esau eventually accepts the flocks. Then

Esau's all like, let's get on our way, and I'll accompany you.

Then, Jacob's all like, nah it's cool, I've got baby animals and children and shit, can't travel fast, blah blah blah, you go on ahead, I'll catch up. It seems a little bit suss to me. Jacob's probably thinking along the lines of, "never try to scam a scammer" and smells a rat, perhaps. Wants to take it slow and let Esau show his hand, as it were. Esau offers to leave some of his mates behind with them, and Jacob's all like, dude, why do that? Let me just go along in the Lord's favour… sounding more and more desperate to get rid of Esau and his entourage with every passing second, despite heading in that general direction anyway. Of course, if Jacob hadn't swindled Esau out of his birthright and his father's blessing, he wouldn't have every single panic alarm inside his head screaming at him like Admiral Ackbar. Finally Esau relented and went on ahead to Seir; however Jacob, the conniving, snivelling little weasel he is, hightailed it to Sukkoth, where he sheltered himself and his livestock, before hoofing it over to Shechem and *purchasing* (I know, right?!) a plot of land and building within sight of the city, set up another altar and called it El Elohe Israel.

Amusing side note here: When Jacob when to Sukkoth to secure his flocks, the bible then quotes, *"That is why the place is called Sukkoth."*

*(Gen. 33:17)*. Sukkoth, in the Hebrew, is the name for a religious thanksgiving celebration, although it's also generally accepted to have been a place. Question is, was Sukkoth a place BEFORE Jacob got there, or did he just arbitrarily name it that when he rocked up? Does Sukkoth in ancient Hebrew actually mean, "Thank Fuck I Managed To Avoid Esau's Revenge Trap And Wow This Looks Like A Good Spot To Hide Out While I Plan My Next Move" (or equivalent)? I guess, not being fluent in ancient Hebrew, I will never know, but it sounds about right.

## Genesis 34: The Downfall of the Shechemites, because of a Dinah-Tap

*"Men are more prone to revenge injuries than to requite kindness." –Thomas Fuller.*

Here we find the lovely Troy-esque story of Dinah, daughter of Leah and Jacob. Apparently she went out one day to visit the women in the land, and whilst on her travels caught the eye of Shechem, son of Hamor the Hivite, who summarily raped the girl (Gen. 34:2). Followed incongruously by, *"His heart was drawn to Dinah daughter of Jacob; he loved the young woman and spoke tenderly to her." (Gen. 34:3)*. Dude, you just RAPED the girl like a mindless animal; I think it's a little late for her to respond positively to tender words, don't you? Still, he loped back to his father Hamor and asked him to *"get me this girl for my wife."* Of course, rapes don't generally go unnoticed, and Jacob soon got wind of his daughter's defilement, and the sons soon after. Meanwhile Hamor went out to talk with Jacob concerning his own son's uncontrolled desires.

The Camp of Jacob was, of course, shocked and furious, because it was counted an "outrageous thing" that Shechem had done, sleeping with Jacob's daughter – *"a thing that should not be done" (Gen. 34:7)*. Well, firstly I wouldn't put "sleeping with" in the same category as "raping" – although the mechanics are basically the same, there is an element of mutual consent missing in the latter term – and secondly, I'm not entirely sure whether it's the rape itself that was offensive, so much as it was rape by someone not of the Jacob family. I would hazard a guess that if Jacob himself had forced himself on the girl, there wouldn't have been so much as a batted eyelid; but because it was someone outside the family, watering down those batshit crazy bloodlines, the howls of outrage erupted in earnest.

So Hamor has treated with the Jacob tribe, asking for Dinah for Shechem's wife, inviting them to intermarry with his tribe, to settle, live, trade and even acquire property in his lands. Shechem adds his two shekels' worth, declaring he will do whatever the Jacob tribe asks, only that he should have Dinah for his wife. (Gen. 34:10 – 34:12). The sons of Jacob, however are still extremely pissed about the whole rape thing (probably because she's unclean, and unavailable for them now) and, learning well from their weasel father, treat deceitfully with Hamor and Shechem. They tell them that *"we can't give our sister to a man who is not circumcised. That would be a disgrace to us." (Gen. 34:14)*. They then propose a deal where the Hivites would circumcise all of their males, the Jacobites would then intermarry with them and live as one with them and all that other shit I said before (do I see a panicky Admiral Ackbar waving frantically in the background, desperate for our attention?).

Hamor and Shechem think this is a great idea, mostly I think because they're thinking with the wrong heads – they'll be thinking a great deal more about them soon enough - and agree to this deal, and lost no time in hacking at the genitalia of every male in the city. Then three days later, whilst the Hivites were still incapacitated from their collective bob jobs, Jacob's brothers Simeon and Levi grabbed their swords and attacked the unsuspecting city, slaughtering every man they encountered, including the hapless Hamor and Shechem, looted the city of all its women, children, goods and livestock and retrieved Dinah. When he heard, Jacob was uncharacteristically mortified, and berated the brothers for *"making me obnoxious to the Canaanites and Perizzites, the people living in this land." (Gen. 34:30)*. To which the brothers asked if the Hivites should have treated their sister like a prostitute. A fair call, I suppose, but genocidal retribution, callously executed, for the defilement of one woman is overreacting just a tiny little bit. It's like killing a mosquito with a sledgehammer; it's possible, but is it necessary? Again I ask you, dear readers: are these the kinds of lessons and behaviours we should be teaching our children? It might be a different story if, after lying, cheating and murdering their way through great swathes of the ancient world, Jacob and his tribe suddenly contracted an aggressive cancer and died horribly because that's what happens if you don't treat people with kindness and respect. If the bible's prime purpose is to control the masses through fear, then this would be a great way to ensure capitulation. But so far these amoral arsehats have gotten off scot-free, and with all their ill-gotten gains intact. Hardly the sort of lesson to inspire people to behave properly. Is it really any surprise why religious sects today, who are similar in every single way bar one or two minor differences, are willing to kill each other (or at the very least, ostracize their followers socially, financially and in every other way) purely for those minor differences? I personally have seen this in action, where a certain religious faction in the workplace has discriminated against one of their own countrymen quite harshly, purely because he followed a slightly different religion. Same Christian values, mind you, but just a slightly different approach, was enough to justify the sanctions. Hardly seems "Christian" to me, but then I think the whole lot is a crock of shit, so I'm hardly in a position to understand how such a minute difference can be so grievously offensive to the opposing factions. Never mind, it's certainly not the last time we'll see such blatant self-serving behaviours in this so-called Book of Guiding Morals. Let us press on, and see just how low they can go.

## Genesis 35: Jacob slinks off, God covers the Rear

*"Insanity runs in my family. It practically gallops."*
– Cary Grant.

Straight into our chapter, God tells Jacob to hightail it to Bethel, to settle there and to build an altar to him (even though he built one there when he was running from Esau's murderous wrath back in Gen. 28). Jacob then gathers his tribe and tells them to get rid of their "foreign gods" (again, probably those soothsaying teraphim similar to the ones Rachel stole from her father), which they did as well as *"the rings in their ears"* (Gen. 35:4) and he buried the lot under an oak tree at Shechem. Who knows why the earrings had to go, unless it had something to do with "purifying themselves" prior to the journey; but unless they were going to walk through a lightning storm, there was hardly any need to get rid of them. I suppose by this stage the tribe were just trying to keep Jacob happy, especially when he was inclined to take a knife to their genitalia when he wasn't. For whatever reason, this was done, and Jacob drags the whole sorry lot of them back to Bethel, during which journey we're told that the *"terror of God fell upon the towns all around them so that no one pursued them"* (Gen. 35:5). Of course, this would not have been necessary on God's part had Jacob not been such an amoral, murderous prick, but if history has shown us anything it's that having friends in high places is one of the biggest keys to success in any endeavour.

So they get to Bethel, Jacob builds an altar (well, *another* altar) and called it El Bethel. Then a whole bunch of random shit happens, including the death of Rebekah's nurse named Deborah, who was buried under another oak tree which was called Allon Bakuth (I swear they're making it up as they go along: well, I tend to think that anyway, but in this particular instance, more so). Then when Jacob returns from Paddan Aram, he gets another visit from God who opines, *"Your name is Jacob, but you will no longer be called Jacob; your name will be Israel."* (Gen. 35:10). Ugh... didn't God already rename Jacob as Israel back in Gen. 32 when they had their quasi-homosexual wrestling match, and God cheated by touching Jacob inappropriately? Was it really necessary for him to make a return trip to reinforce the issue? Why was it so important for Jacob to be re-named Israel? What, indeed, was the point of the exercise? If you ask me, God's got some serious issues, not least among them being substandard memory faculties.

Anyway, after this re-renaming business, God starts again with the be fruitful and increase in number and nations will rise from your loins and kings will be your descendants and blah blah blah, and all the land I gave illegitimately to Abe and Isaac I give to you now and so on and so forth, before he "went up from Jacob, Israel, whatever", as a result of which Jacob, Israel, whatever made another pillar and made a drink offering on it, and poured oil on it, then named the place Bethel, despite it already being called that, otherwise God couldn't have instructed Jacob to go there in the first place. See, NOW we're talking with the drink offerings; in fact, as a God, I would like to have drink offerings placed on altars for me, preferably rum of course, but I'd pass on the oil unless I needed to service the car. But it's hard to rename a place Bethel when it's already been called that. And in all likelihood, Jisrael probably poured dirty camel water on the pillar instead of a decent rum which any god worth their salt pillars would enjoy. Times were hard back then.

**Isaac and Rachel kick the bucket**

The second half of this Genesis chapter goes on to say how Rachel died during childbirth, with a son she named Ben-Oni, and whom *"his father"* renamed Benjamin (Gen. 35:18). Interesting how they used "his father" instead of, say, Issac. It rather makes me wonder why they would choose to word it that way, when the identity of the father was known; or was it? No matter. They buried her on the way to Ephrath (Bethlehem), Jacob (back to Jacob again) set up another pillar which *"to this day"* (apparently) marks Rachel's tomb. Be that as it may; I am certainly not denying that *someone* named Rachel was buried there, and that she was married to someone called Isaac, and that these roamings occurred more or less as put down in the bible. What IS up to debate is the existence of this God character, and why he's meddling in our affairs, changing our names, committing real estate fraud, alternatively drowning people and saving them, then getting them to mutilate their own sex parts -  the list goes on and on and on. If there IS a supreme being that created us all, he is clearly not right in the head. Omnipotent, omniscient, omnipresent, and as mentally stable as a one legged tightrope walker on a pogo stick.

But I digress. Israel (back to Israel now, but this gets interchanged with Jacob with dizzying regularity – let's just settle for Jisrael, okay?) heads for, and pitches his tent, "beyond Migdar Eder" wherever that is, during which time Reuben sleeps with his father's concubine Bilhah (which, if you recall from Gen. 30 was actually spelled Bilbah – another deity-enforced name-change perhaps?) which Jisrael "heard about" (but never seemed to *do* anything about). It then lists Jisrael's twelve sons, which I shall gloss over unless it becomes relevant later, listed in birth order according to whether it was Leah's, Rachel's, Bilhah's (nee Bilbah) or Zilphah's. Finally, the bible relates how Jisrael came home to his father Isaac in Mamre (you know, that old swindling bastard that mistakenly gave Esau's blessing to Jacob *on his deathbed* back in Genesis 27, but has somehow managed to live at least fourteen or fifteen more years, at best estimate, in this condition). He finally kicks the bucket though, and he is buried by his sons Jacob and Esau, who seem to have mended their differences, or at the least have called a truce until the funeral is over.

## Genesis 36: The Magnificent Esau and his Incredibly Boring Lineage

*"What's wrong with being a boring kind of guy?" – George H. W. Bush.*

This chapter is one I will eagerly gloss over as minimally as possible, as it merely lists all of Esau's descendants, from his respective wives and concubines and so on and so forth down the line. It is eye-wateringly boring in the extreme except to historical genealogists, who have their own set of intensely personal issues. If you're so inclined, please feel free to go ahead and peruse your nearest bible for the Esau bloodlines, but it is pretty boring stuff for the simple fact that:

a) there's an extensive tongue-twisting list of them; and
b) there are no indications of inbreeding anywhere in Esau's bloodlines, unlike a certain ambiguously-named brother we could mention.

The only immediately interesting things of note are that one of Esau's wives was granddaughter of a Hivite (the people whose males were tricked into genital self-mutilation, then brutally murdered by Jacob's lot) and that this particular wife's father apparently discovered a hot spring. In the words of Austin Powers, "That's. About. It." Moving on then…

## Genesis 37: Joseph's phallic dreams spawn sheaf envy

*"The smaller the mind, the greater the conceit."* – Aesop.

Joseph, who you will recall was the first son of Jacob/Israel/whatever and Rachel, is seventeen at this juncture, and was tending the tribe's stolen livestock with his brothers (the sons of Bilhah/Bilbah/whatever and Zilpah, when he apparently *"brought their father a bad report about them" (Gen. 37:2)*. Sibling rivalry at its best, to be sure, although Joseph benefits from a double-dose of bad blood, inheriting the genetic traits of both Jacob/Israel/whatever AND Rebekah, so I suppose he never really stood any chance of developing normally. In a lot of respects, it's like watching some of the "reality shows" we're inundated with constantly, such as Survivor or Big Brother, where being cunning and underhanded is key to survival; but if you're perceived as being *too* cunning, the rest of the weaker tribe members will unfailingly band together to eliminate the Alpha threat. Such is the case with Joseph, who is undisputedly Jacob/Israel/whatever's favourite child, having been the firstborn from Rachel's mostly barren loins.

Joseph, for his part, only makes matters worse for himself when he starts to experience vivid dream imagery. In and of itself, it's no big deal, except that he chooses to "share" it with his brothers (in essence, rub their faces in the fact that he's the favourite child). He is already hated because he was gifted with an ornate robe that itself becomes a symbol of preferential treatment, so when he starts sharing these dreams of his, the resentment swells. In one dream, he relates, *"We were binding sheaves of grain out in the field and my suddenly my sheaf rose and stood upright, while your sheaves gathered around mine and bowed down to it." (Gen. 37:7).* Now, ignoring the blatantly phallic implications of the dream which would inspire Freud to spend some Alone Time with his mother, it's obvious that this dream is an unconscious visualization of the conscious mind's knowledge that he is the Golden Child who will most likely inherit everything. It's no wonder his less loved brothers wanted to crease his skull with a shovel. This was further compounded when Joseph related another of his "visions" whereby he dreamed that, *"the sun and moon and eleven stars were bowing down to me" (Gen. 37:9).* Again, pretty obvious to work out: the sun and moon meaning his parents, and eleven siblings, bowing down to him and his hyper-inflated ego. Of course, nothing good can come of this, as sure as pride comes before a fall.

Some time later, Jacob/Israel/whatever calls Joseph, and sends him off to find his brothers who are currently tending the flocks near

Shechem, to see that all is well, and report back (Gen. 37:14). By the time Joseph arrives there, however, his brothers and the flocks they're tending have moved on, and a brief enquiry to a wandering man results in Joseph eventually finding them at Dothan. Joseph's brothers, however, see Joseph approaching them in the distance and, noses firmly out-of-joint, plotted to kill him.

The first idea was to throw Joseph into one of the cisterns (new exciting word! Apparently "wells" is out of vogue) and claim that a large predatory animal devoured him. *"Then we'll see what comes of his dreams" (Gen. 37:20).* Sounds a little bit like that Israeli fighter with the shiny dentition in the Van Damme movie Bloodsport: *"Now I show YOU some trick or two...!!"* Excuse me while I literally Laugh Out Loud– such an awesome movie though, sit down and watch it with your kids today! Reuben, however, is getting cold feet about the impending fratricide and implores his brothers to just chuck him in the cistern but not harm him, intending to rescue Joseph at a safe time and return him to his father. So when Joseph finally reached his brothers, they stripped him of his ornate robe, chucked him in the nearest dry cistern, and sat down to eat (Gen. 37:23).

Whilst enjoying their repast, they spotted a caravan of Ishmaelites coming from, apparently, Gilead (Ishmaelites, of course, descending from Ishmael of Hagar fame, the Egyptian slave-concubine thingy of Crazy Old Abe's wife Sarai/Sarah/whatever. Related after a fashion, what we today might call a prick-relation). Seeing that the Ishmaelites were on their way to Egypt to flog off their spices and balms and myrrh and shit, the brother Judah (I know, right?!) suggests that instead of killing their brother Joseph, they should sell him into slavery. They brothers agree, and when the merchants arrive, they haul Joseph's sorry arse out of the well (sorry, cistern) and flog him off for twenty shekels of silver, whereupon Joseph gets shipped off to Egypt.

Quick sidenote: How coincidental is this, by the way:

- Judah = sells his brother to the Ishmaelites for 20 shekels of silver for being a pompous prick;
- Judas = sells his saviour to the Romans for 30 shekels of silver for calling him out in front of the gang.

Sounds incredibly similar to me, almost the same names and the same situation, with a slightly inflated price. An intriguing example of repeated history, I will leave it here purely for entertainment purposes. For now, back to the story. Reuben returns and, finding the well empty of both water and brother, *"tears his clothes" (Gen. 37:29)*. Strange thing to do, if you ask me, unless it means moistening them with liquid from his eyeballs rather than rending them in a violent fashion. He finds his brothers and asks for guidance, whereupon they slaughtered a goat and dipped Joseph's ornate robe in the blood. They then returned to their father claiming they "found" the robe and asked him to examine it (Gen. 37:32). Quite obviously, Jacob/Israel/whatever immediately recognizes the ornate robe, and assumes that his Golden

Child has been eaten by a ferocious animal, and torn to pieces. He tears his robe (as in violently rends this time), puts a sack on and mourns the loss of his son for the rest of his days. Meanwhile, the hapless (and humbled) Joseph has been flogged off to Potiphar, who it turns out is captain of the guard to the Egyptian pharaoh.

## Genesis 38: To Er is human, to wank divine

*"If you think you're having a bad day, just picture a T-Rex trying to masturbate." – Rotten e-card.*

After the nastiness of attempted fratricide, Judah left his brothers and ended up marrying the daughter of some Canaanite dude, and ended up with three sons, named Er, Onan, and Shelah. Later on (no time frame specified), Judah scored a wife for Er called Tamar. However, Er was *"wicked in the LORD's sight, and so the LORD put him to death" (Gen. 38:7)*. So now we encounter a subtle change in man/deity relationships. No longer "God" but "LORD" in big, blocky capital letters. There is no reason for this; no fanfare, no God coming down to his fave peeps and declaring, "I am your God, but I am no longer your God. I am now the LORD" or some equally-confusing immortal bullshit brain-fart, no nothing. Just a random renaming for no discernible reason. Perhaps Team Leader Yaweh finally kicked the bucket (or more likely, was institutionalized) by this stage, and the celestial expedition abruptly came under new management. It's no different to when you have a "Team Leader" who suddenly becomes an "Operational Supervisor" with a bigger pay packet but the same breathtaking lack of competency.

Anyway, Judah tries to salvage the situation by telling second son Onan to "do his duty" and sleep with his brother's wife/widow. Onan, however, gets the idea in his head that if he sleeps with Tamar, any children conceived with her won't be "his" but his brother's (nobody said they were smart back then) so whenever he slept with Tamar, he *"spilled his semen on the ground to keep from providing offspring for his brother" (Onanism, Gen. 38:9)*. So there you have it, you single guys who are lonely and frustrated, yet guilt-laden and scared of eternal hell for all those date-nights with Mrs. Palmer and her five daughters. Onanism, or "spilling the seed" is only a sin if you're trying to avoid getting your brother's wife pregnant by pulling out, and has nothing to do with batting off to Playmate of the Month. Of course, the church and organized religion will still attempt to use this passage to generate guilt in the unwary and, through offers of "salvation", will gain another mindless sheep for their flock (and the monies fleeced via collection plate). But now, with your newfound knowledge of where the term originates, you can call their prudish bluff with confidence.

Okay, so: Onan. Didn't want his semen used to have his brother's children (I still boggle at this astounding ignorance of how genetics works), and spills it on the ground. Apparently this is also wicked in the LORD's sight, and he was put to death as well (Gen. 38:10). No, don't panic single guys, stay strong! One person who *is* panicking, however, is Judah, who implores Tamar to remain a widow in her father's household until his third son Shelah grows up, fearing that Shelah will follow the fate of his brothers. Seems like a reasonable assumption to me: God (sorry, THE LORD) is already pissed with your family and snuffed two of your offspring; odds are good that he'll hit the trifecta eventually. So as a father you take the necessary precautions, such as you can take against a deity/astral traveler when all you have to protect yourself is sand and goat shit. And so Tamar gets choofed off to her father, and time passes for an indeterminate period of, well, time.

Enough time it would seem for Judah's wife to eventually kick the bucket. After his period of mourning Judah heads up to Tinmah to help shear some sheep, apparently. The crux of the story is that Tamar gets wind of Judah's working junket and, after shedding all of her widow's clothing and donning a veil, sat herself at Enaim, which is allegedly somewhere on the way to Tinmah. The idea here is that Tamar has noticed that third son Shelah is now grown up but she hasn't yet been given to him as wife, or something. It seems stupid that she should do this, because there is no mention of Shelah actually accompanying his father on this working junket; according to the bible it was Judah's mate Hirah the Adullamite that went with him.

"Wait, wait…. what the hell is an Adullamite?!" I hear you ask stridently. Well, if you ignore its "original" usage as, "a member of a dissident political group (originally applied to a group of British MPs who seceded from the Liberal party in 1866), my old mate Google has described its origins as, *"adopted in allusion to the cave of Adullam, where those discontented with the rule of Saul came to join David (1 Sam. 22:1-2)."* In a nutshell, it describes a group of distressed, indebted and/or discontented individuals who were hiding in a cave and who had rallied around a dodgy fucker by the name of David who had a penchant for braining taller people with rocks flung from a sling. Presumably, this adoption took place after the rock-slinging incident, which certain religionists like to place somewhere around 1020 B.C. What interests me, though, is that there's been no mention of Samuel, nor his book, until now. We're still trying to wade our way through Genesis and we're already getting references to other passages from other points of view. "Confusing" is just the tip of this very enigmatic, discombobulating iceberg, considering we're unable to pin down definitive dates and times for these events. I mean honestly, these are supposed to be the written records of our earliest history, and we can't even pinpoint when these events occurred. We're supposed to swallow the idea that Noah emerged from his ark on the first day of the first month of his 601$^{st}$ year (Gen. 8:13), and yet, so many years down the track, humans have somehow lost the ability to reliably time-stamp these momentous events in history?

"Well, yeah, but what about the Tower of Babel?" I hear the faithful screaming. Humanity got swatted to the four winds and had all their language scrambled, they reason. Well, sure, but their basic cognitive skills were still intact. They didn't forget how to breathe or rationalize or tend flocks or timekeep; the only thing that's changed is the language in which they're keeping it. Honestly, ancient record-keeping dudes, something as simple as a date (say, for example, 305 A.F. – After Flood) would have been marvelous and saved all of us up here in the future a lot of confusion and dis-agreement.

Anyway, back to Tamar. Dons a veil to conceal her identity and way-lays Judah on the way to Tinmah, for what reason we are yet to fathom. On their meeting, however, Judah mistakes this veiled female for a wandering prostitute and propositions her for sex. A deal was made concerning the promise of a goat and the keeping of a seal and cord and staff as surety and, long story short, got pregnant to her father-in-law (Gen. 38:15 – 38:18). Okay firstly, if you wanted to find out what was happening with your supposedly arranged marriage, why would you go in disguise? Secondly, if that disguise led your father-in-law to believe you were a prostitute, wouldn't logic and personal dignity dictate that you would promptly dispel the man of that impression? Instead we're given a reinforcement of the old adage that there's a bit of a whore in everyone. After this deed, she hightails it back home and returns to her mourning clothes, plus one staff, one seal, one cord and one bun in the oven, but still minus any answer to the question she went out for in the first place. Mind-boggling. Of course, Judah for his part sends this promised goat back to the shrine with his Adullamite mate to complete the transaction, only to discover this mysterious "shrine prostitute" is nowhere to be found, nor was there ever a shrine prostitute, according to one of the locals.

Three months later, and it's brought to Judah's attention that his daughter-in-law is pregnant and guilty of prostitution. He summarily commands she be "brought out" and burned to death (Gen. 38:24). As she was being brought out, she "sent a message" to her father-in-law (I suppose, through her captors prior to being brought before him), saying that she was pregnant to the man who owns – you guessed it – the seal, cord and staff. Judah of course recognized these things as his own and proclaims (I boggle to repeat it): *"She is more righteous than I, since I wouldn't give her to my son Shelah." (Gen. 38:26)*. A truly mind-blowing statement. She deliberately dressed as a prostitute, concealed her identity, laid in wait for her father-in-law at Enaim, and sold her arse to him for a goat, and *she* is the person with the moral high ground here? Just how bad are Judah's morals that he considers Tamar superior in that department? He had sex with (he thought) a prostitute for a goat. Well whoop-de do, it's not like he had sex with the goat, although in some religions that's considered permissible and, apparently, preferable. Anyway, Judah doesn't sleep with is daughter-in-law again, and when she goes into labour it turns out there are twins. One of the kids sticks a hand out (just a hand, how messed up is that?) and the midwife tied a scarlet thread around it, to indicate first-born status. But then the hand retreats (equally messed up) and the other twin emerges first, followed by Scarlet Thread. The boys are named Perez and Zerah respectively.

It seems a strange thing to put into a religious book, the Tale of the Reaching Hand, but I'm sure the author had a reason for including it that will make itself apparent later. And it makes me wonder once again who, exactly, is writing all this stuff down in the first place, and why. Is the bible a true and accurate record of the events of early humanity, physically-impossible events notwithstanding? Is it just a record of one particular dynasty - to whit, the descendants of Noah – and his family history, although for a family so devoid of basic morals it seems strange that they would want to immortalize those acts for perpetuity. Is it the writings of one of God's lackeys (angels for wont of a better description) observing all the goings-on and recording them? Are they merely the fevered scrawlings of a disturbed mind, trying to make sense of powers beyond his comprehension as God or Team Leader Yaweh or whoever exercises that power over his genetic experiments? We weren't there, so I suppose we shall never truly know which one it is. What we can say for certain is that humanity has a long, long way to go before being enlightened enough to achieve global harmony, and treating the bible as a guide to the way we're supposed to live is so counter-productive to that goal that we are actually regressing as a species. The acts of terrorism committed in the name of religion today are despicable in the extreme, the complete capitulation of rational thought seen on the faces of parishioners in the super-churches, being fleeced of their money for the unfulfilled promise of a pair of wings and a harp, or 72 virgins, or whatever else it is being promised for toeing the line on the earthly plane. And all because a few undoubtedly charismatic but otherwise psychotic individuals have convinced people of the existence of an invisible man in the sky who watches everyone, everywhere, their whole life, just waiting for them to "sin" so that he can smite them or punish them or some other rubbish so they'd just better bloody well behave, or ELSE!! Really, my loyal readers, haven't we evolved beyond the need for these childish threats? Aren't we, broadly speaking, rational enough in our everyday lives that we can distinguish right from wrong, psychopathic conditions notwithstanding? A simple effort every day to become a better, more tolerant person would go a long way towards global harmony and, if nothing else, will improve your standing with those immediately around you. What have you got to lose?

## Genesis 39: Damned if you do, damned if you don't

*"Heaven hath no rage like love to hatred turned, nor hell a fury like a woman scorned. "* –William Congreve.

We turn our attention back to Joseph (brother of Judah) in this particular chapter, who was sold into slavery to Potiphar, one of the Pharaoh's officials, for his phallic wheat-sheaf dreams and generally thinking he was above the rest of his family. I suppose if you consider they sold their own family member for twenty shekels, you can forgive Joseph for coming to this conclusion. Anyway, we're told the THE LORD is with Joseph and he prospered, and he lived in his master's house. Exactly how a slave can prosper when, in fact, a slave is something that is not elaborated on here. "Prosper" to the average person means to accumulate wealth, have offspring, and generally get ahead in life, and none of these descriptions can be comfortably reconciled with the concept of slavery. But however he managed to prosper within its limited boundaries, Joseph did it. Potiphar saw that Joseph was favoured with THE LORD, and entrusted all his worldly things to him to run and maintain and whatever, whilst Potiphar essentially limited his concentration to his next meal (Gen. 39:6).

At this stage, we are told that Joseph is a handsome bastard indeed, and is "well-built". This attracts the inevitable carnal attentions of Potiphar's wife, who soon put the hard work on our boy Joseph, imploring him to, "Come to bed with me!" in that age-old plea of the sex-deprived wife. Joseph, to his credit, refuses her advances, explaining that he's in a nice, powerful position and asks, *"How then could I do such a wicked thing and sin against God?" (Gen. 39:9)*. Well, firstly Joseph, your sin would be against your owner, not God. There aren't any stone tablets yet, so until then you're essentially on your own moral platform, as unstable as it is. Secondly, if your master holds you in such esteem and his missus is cracking onto you, the first port of call would be to your master to let him know what's going on before shit turns ugly. He's entrusted all his household affairs to you, Joseph, so upfront honesty is going to be appreciated more than trying to spare the master's feelings, which essentially amounts to keeping the poor bastard in the dark while inappropriate things are happening around him. Basic Decency 101 right there, dude.

This sexual harassment occurs for days on end, until one day Joseph enters the house to attend his duties and notices that there are no other servants around. Potiphar's sex-starved missus then ambushes Joseph by grabbing his cloak and imploring him to sleep with her, but he manages to get out of his cloak and run from the house. This, of course, pisses off the frustrated woman, who then calls for her servants and screams, *"Look, this Hebrew has been brought to us to make sport of us! He came in here to sleep with me, but I screamed. When he heard me scream for help, he left his cloak beside me and ran out of the house." (Gen. 39:14 – 39:16).* Needless to say, the nasty piece of work waited for Potiphar to get home and told him the same cock-and-bull story, getting Joseph in a whole pile of shit. Potiphar kicked Joseph into prison, with the King's prisoners.

*"But THE LORD was with him; he showed him kindness and granted him favour in the eyes of the prison warden" (Gen. 39:21).* Please excuse me while I literally "LOL" here; if that was even remotely true, Joseph wouldn't be in prison (let alone get sold into slavery by his brothers) in the first place. He'd be kicking along elsewhere tending his flocks and shit, with no physical or mental health problems, a smoking hot wife or seven, a couple of sprogs, and all the gold he could eat. A person blessed by THE LORD wouldn't – shouldn't - find himself in the situation Joseph is in; and if that's the definition of "being blessed", then I most certainly want no part of it, thank you very much. Anyway, the same thing applies to this warden as it did for Potiphar, in that he put Joseph in charge of all the prisoners and whatever, and *"paid no attention to anything under Joseph's care" (Gen. 39:23)*, because THE LORD was with him and blah blah blah. I would instead suppose that, in addition to having a superiority complex, Joseph was also very charismatic in a manner that he was able to manipulate the people he met into letting him do his own thing. Such an ability to twist people around your little finger might well be seen as being "blessed" by some deity, all the sold-into-slavery and being imprisoned notwithstanding.

## Genesis 40: Joseph the Soothsayer turns Pagan, interprets Dreams

*"Properly speaking, the unconscious is the real psychic; its inner nature is just as unknown to us as the reality of the external world, and it is just as imperfectly reported to us through the data of consciousness as is the external world through the indications of our sensory organs."* – Sigmund Freud, The Interpretation of Dreams.

Some time later, we are told, the Pharaoh's cupbearer and his baker pissed him off enough to be sent to the prison Joseph has been essentially running for the prison warden. No indication of how much time, mind you, could have been a couple of hours, days, weeks, months, who can tell? For the nonce, we'll read that they were incarcerated, and the warden placed these two into Joseph's care, who then tended whatever needs to which they were entitled (Gen. 40:1- 40:4). Well and good so far. Then, after the pair had been in Pharaoh's custody "for some time" (again, no specific timeframe), both of these ex-officials had a dream, each with a meaning of their own; yet without anyone available to interpret the dreams, they got all depressed and dejected about it. (Gen. 40:5 – 40:7).

Enter Joseph, Soothsayer Extraordinaire, who of all people in the bible should know that interpreting dreams on the fly can result in some

Serious Unpleasantness, if you're lucky. He asks why the two guys are so sad, and they divulge their respective dreams to him. The cupbearer tells of a dream of a vine with three branches, which flowered and fruited, which he squeezed into a cup, then giving the filled cup to the Pharaoh. Joseph told the cupbearer that, in three days, the Pharaoh will restore the man to his former position, but that when it happens, that he must remember Joseph, and mention him to the Pharaoh and get him out of prison (which he promises).

The baker observes this interpretation, and tells Joseph of his dream of three baskets of bread and baked goods for the Pharaoh on his head, but birds were eating the bread in the middle one. Joseph interpreted this one *slightly* differently, however. He told the baker that in three days the Pharaoh would lift the baker's head from his body and that the birds would eat the flesh from his body.

So it turns out that, three days later, it was the Pharaoh's birthday. Hmm. Joseph, slave to one of Pharaoh's officials, didn't know that it was Pharaoh's birthday in three days' time? Most unlikely. Anyway, it turns out that the cupbearer was restored to his position and the baker was impaled on a pole. Yeah right: lucky guess, Joseph, although I can't help but feel you had some insider information about the fates of those two hapless servants; after all, you're essentially running the whole damn prison for the lazy-arsed warden, so you would undoubtedly be privy to why they were sent to prison in the first place, and what punishments were going to be meted out, AND when. It's all part of the Politics of Ruling, you know. Pharaoh has a great big Cake Day celebration, but of course he can't have that without booze, and the cupbearer's crime was probably nothing worse than giving the bugger a cup of watered-down wine, which may not have even been his fault, whereas the baker might have grabbed the Ratsak instead of the flour and poisoned one of the Pharaoh's rellies. So in a magnificent example of political acumen, the Pharaoh uses his Cake Day celebrations to bring the two hapless servants up, forgives one of them to show mercy and kindness, and executes the other as a lesson to the others; everyone at the party witnesses this, and goes around telling everyone they meet that the Pharaoh is "firm, but fair" with his dealing of crime and justice. Clever, savvy Pharaoh..!

The cupbearer, however, neglects to mention Joseph to the pharaoh, and forgets him. That's gratitude for you, isn't it, although anyone in the cupbearer's position would probably be deep in the cups himself celebrating his good fortune in avoiding Death by Sharp Stick, and we all know how those vitally important things we meant to say seem to disappear with a steady flow of alcohol. And so Joseph remains in prison, for the interim.

## Genesis 41: Pharaoh Dreams, summons Joseph the Soothsayer

*"In the matter of boots, I defer to the authority of the boot-maker." –Mikhail Bakunin.*

We pick up our story a full two years after the events of Genesis 40, at which time the Pharaoh himself has a dream, or rather, a series of them with a recurring theme. The first dreamscape being him standing next to the Nile and watching seven fat, healthy cows emerge from the waters; these were followed by seven gaunt, ugly cows which then ate the healthy cows (Gen. 41:1 – 41:4). Briefly awakening and subsiding back into slumber, a similar vision was dreamed, but with a wheat sheaf with seven healthy heads being "eaten" by seven desiccated wheat heads (how a head of wheat eats another head of wheat is beyond me, but then dreams don't always have to make sense). On waking in the morning, the Pharaoh sent off for any and all magicians, soothsayers and such mystic creatures who might be able to interpret the dreams he had (Gen. 41:5 – 41:8).

It was at this stage that the cupbearer piped up and, recalling his promise to Joseph, informed the Pharaoh of his experience during his incarceration. Pharaoh sent for Joseph to be brought to him immediately and so, after being cleaned up somewhat, Joseph was dragged in before the Pharaoh (Gen. 41:8 – 41:14). The Pharaoh told

Joseph that he had some dreams, and had heard how Joseph had correctly interpreted the dreams of the two officials in his prison. Joseph replied, *"I cannot do it, but God will give Pharaoh the answer he desires" (Gen 41:15 – 41:16)*. Clever, wily Joseph. Caught with his pants down, and with no prior information available to cold-read the Pharaoh's dreams, he quickly deferred responsibility – and therefore, liability – for any dream interpretations onto God, implying that he, Joseph, is merely the messenger, and please don't shoot the messenger (or in his case, imprison and impale the messenger). Nice deflection work, there.

So Pharaoh relates his dream imagery and asks Joseph what it all means. Joseph proclaims that the dreams all mean the same thing (not much of a stretch there). The seven cows and the seven heads of grain both relate to seven years, therefore he prophesizes that there will be seven years of abundance, followed by seven years of famine. He went on and asserted that the similar meanings meant that *"the matter has been firmly decided by God, and God will do it soon" (Gen. 41:32)*. Finally, Joseph recommended Pharaoh find a "discerning and wise man", put him in charge of Egypt, and that the Pharaoh keep one fifth of all food production in reserve to help protect Egypt from this imminent famine.

The Pharaoh finds all this to his liking, and who do you think he chooses for his "discerning and wise man" to run things? Why, our old mate Joseph, who has the ear of God and is therefore the most discerning and wise of them all. He summarily appoints Joseph second in power only to him, and hands over control of all Egypt.

The. Mind. Boggles. What ruler in their right mind would do such a thing? I'm sure there were many superstitious people back in the day, but can we seriously expect that the ruling class of Egypt are so inept that they would not provide a means of securing the food of their country? They built the bloody pyramids, after all, so surely a couple of grain silos wasn't entirely out of the question, yeah? Imagine for a moment that the President of the United States had a dream, and he wanted it interpreted, and that as the result of a favour you did someone you were released from prison to interpret this dream, after which you were given the United States to control. *It would never happen*, not even with Donald Trump in the chair! It is so fundamentally against every example of rational human behaviour that we must discount this story as pure fallacy, unless of course Pharaoh was brain damaged, or a five-year-old child.

Consulting what archaeologists have discovered regarding ancient Egyptian history, there was indeed a seven-year period of famine in the country during the reign of King Djoser called the Famine Stele, in an inscription from the Ptolemaic Dynasty dated approximately 330 BCE (Before Common Era, essentially the same as B.C.), long after Djoser's reign which Is dated around 2686 B.C. when upper and lower Egypt were united into a single kingdom. So we know through these inscriptions that a famine of this magnitude did occur, however there is no mention of some Hebrew slave predicting this famine and being given control of Egypt as a result. There is a reference of increased tributes to the Egyptian god Khnemu once the famine ended, but of course that was after the famine which is not generally considered prophesy, but more of an *après coup* scenario. Certainly there is nothing concrete in reference to the bible's assertions. It could be that Joseph's blowing his own horn again, although the result this time turned out a little better than the last time he tried it on.

### 2-IC Joseph makes like a Squirrel

Joseph has by some minor miracle gone from a mere Hebrew slave to the second most powerful man in Egypt, if the biblical stories are to be believed, in one fell swoop. Sanctioned by the Pharaoh, dressed in the finest linens, adorned in gold chains and the Pharaoh's own signet ring, Joseph squirrelled away grain "beyond measure" and, when the years of famine fell upon Egypt, opened the storehouses and fed the nation. Apparently, the whole world was coming to buy food from him, as other countries were enjoying their own famine, although it was supposed to have only affected Egypt. How nice of God to share the famine across the world like that, despite only giving dream-like warnings of it to the Pharaoh of Egypt. Because if God was as loving and kind as proponents of the bible suggest, why would he then bring down famines and pain and disease and suffering and so forth? Seems a little hypocritical at best, and sadistic at worst, a regular Stockholm Syndrome thing happening between God and man, "Oh, I'm suffering and in agony, therefore God must really love me..!" Riiiight...

# Genesis 42: Joseph Gets His Own Back, Sort Of

*"Revenge is not a noble trait, but it is a human one." – Rudy Giuliani.*

By this stage of the game, our scaly mate Jacob/Israel/Whatever is also in the grip of the famine and has heard of the food stores in Egypt. He collects his sons and tells them to head off and collect some, *"so that we may live and not die" (Gen. 42:2).* So ten of them shuffled off to Egypt, all except Benjamin, for Jacob felt that his life might be in danger. Therefore Jacob/Israel/whatever sent all his sons bar one to bargain for Egypt's grain, as Canaan was suffering a famine as well.

It still amuses me greatly that God would choose to alert Egypt's ruler to an imminent famine, but not the rulers of other countries and kingdoms. Doubly so when you consider that Jacob/Israel/whatever was firmly in God's pocket for quite a while, so you'd think he would at least have taken time out of his day to piss in his ear at some stage about the need to stock up on non-perishables. Why, I ask, is Jacob/Israel/whatever suddenly on the outer with the G-man? Some inappropriate touching whilst they were "wrestling" by the river would be my guess, but hey, I wasn't there. For what we shall call Reasons Unknown, God has left Jacob/Israel/Whatever to his own devices for a while and kept his omnipresent eyeball on Joseph for the interim.

Anyway, these sons of Jacob/Israel/Whatever hoof it off to Egypt to procure some of this grain, and prostrate themselves in front of Joseph, who by this stage is in charge of all the disseminations of grain and is going by the unlikely name of Zaphenath-Paneah, bestowed on Joseph by the Pharaoh (seriously? I thought God was bad for renaming people, but at least he provided names you could pronounce. What the hell is Zaphenath-Paneah?!?! Call the poor bastard Joe and be done with it, yeah..?). Needless to say, whilst Joseph's brothers did not recognize him, he most certainly recognized them, and summarily accused them of being spies searching for weaknesses in the Egyptian defences. They deny it of course, but Joseph is enjoying his position of power and gets all of them thrown in prison bar one, who is ordered to go back home and return with the remaining brother (Gen. 42:1 – 42:17).

So he puts them all in prison for three days, letting them stew in their own juices as it were. On the third day, Joseph puts forward another ultimatum as the original one isn't gaining much traction with his former brothers: one of the brothers is to remain in prison, while the rest take grain back for their starving households, whilst still maintaining that the youngest brother be brought to him, *"so that your words may be verified and that you may not die" (Gen. 42:18 – 42:20)*. Makes perfect sense, doesn't it, readers? If keeping ALL the brothers in prison and sending one back for the errant brother doesn't work, why not keep ONE in prison and send the rest back with grain, on the promise of bringing the errant brother back? What magnificently mind-altering drugs is he on? Has he forgotten how sadistic his family dynamic was when he was part of the tribe? How they chucked him inna hole and sold him into slavery because of his phallic, I'm-better-than-all-of-you wheat dream?

Anyway, the brothers discussed the matter amongst themselves, reckoning that their current predicament was because of what they'd done to Joseph. Reuben, however, said, *"Didn't I tell you not to sin against the boy? But you wouldn't listen! Now we must give an accounting for his blood." (Gen. 42:22)*. Joseph hears all this of course, but as he was apparently using an interpreter, they were unaware that he could understand their discussions. So Joseph goes away and has a little cry about it, then comes back and binds Simeon in front of his brothers, before providing them with sacks of grain, the silver they brought and their other provisions, and sending them back to Jacob/Israel/whatever.

So off they scoot back to their Father of Changeable Name, on the way back discovering that their silver coins intended to buy the grain had been stored in their grain bags, at which there was much wailing and gnashing of teeth, and lamenting, *"What is this that God has done to us?" (Gen. 42:28)*. Uh, God had nothing to do with it, dipshits, and if you were a little bit more observant you would've twigged that Zaphenath-Paneah was actually your brother Joseph. I mean honestly: after nearly five decades on this planet, I recently discovered I had a brother I knew nothing about, but on meeting the man, I could tell just by looking at him that we were related. There are unmistakable indicators of genetics, facial structure, body build etc. that betray a person's lineage, and yet this pack of idiots couldn't tell their ankle from their arsehole. Whatever. They even-tually return to Jacob/Israel/whatever and tell him everything that transpired on their journey, and the conditions of their return. Jacob/Israel starts the Poor Me thing, saying that Joseph and Simeon had been taken, and now he stands to lose Benjamin, and everything is against me, and blah blah blah, may as well go eat worms. At this point Reuben pipes up and says, *"You may put both of my sons to death if I do not bring him back to you." (Gen. 42:37)*. I understand it's supposed to be an indication of how confident he is in the success of his plans, but such casual disregard for their own family is concerning to me. Who volunteers their own offspring to be put to death for something so trivial as rescuing another family member, honestly? "Oh noes, our brother's being held hostage! Tell you what, dad, if Ben and I don't bring him back, you can kill my sons. Your grandsons." Who in their right mind does that?! Why don't the sons get any say in this? It's their lives on the line. It's bad enough when a family member is being held hostage by an enemy faction, even more so you're the hostage of your own family, your grandfather no less! What is wrong with these people?! This book is supposed to be an example to the reader about good moral fibre, and yet people are taking their own family members hostage, on pain of death! The mind boggles.

Anyway, Jacob/Israel/whatever has the last word on it and says, *"My son will not go down there with you. His brother is dead and he is the only one left. If harm comes to him on the journey you are taking, you will bring my grey head down to the grave in sorrow."* (Gen. 42:38). Um. Firstly, you have twelve sons, not two. Yes, it just so happens that Joseph and Benjamin are the only two sons Rachel gave you, but show some fucking decorum, man! Way to make the others feel valued and loved! By that one statement alone, Jacob/Israel/whatever clearly confirms that his only concerns are the whelps of Rachel, and his other ten children can go and eat camel shit for all he cares. Great parenting, arsehole. From a personal standpoint, if he actually happened to die of sorrow should Benjamin be lost (as he claimed), then the world would have been a much better place for it. There'd be one less self-centred prick to worry about, that's for sure.

## Genesis 43: The Hunger Games

*"Hunger is insolent, and will be fed." –Homer.*

Time passes, and the grain brought back from Egypt by the brothers has been exhausted, so Jacob/Israel/whatever says to his sons, "Go back and buy us a little more food." But Judah – good ol' Judah – reminds his father of what was said to them on the last visit: You will not see my face again unless your brother is with you. (Gen. 43:3). Jizzy gets all upset at this, and asks why they brought all this trouble on him by telling the guy there was another brother. Like it was their fault or something! Again, great role model, he could apply for the Steward of Gondor with that attitude. And the sons are all like, "Dude, he asked us the questions, all we did was answer him. You know, to get food for the family and stuff, how were we to know he'd want to see the other brother, we're not freakin' psychics..!"

Then Judah pipes up and says to his father, *"Send the boy along with me and we will go at once, so that we and you and our children may live and not die." (Gen. 43:8).* Aaaahhh, Jizzy, don't fall for it dude! Ol' Judah's already sold one of the Precious Pair into slavery, and now you're going to hand over the other one? Dangerous ground if you ask me, don't do it! But, of course, there is the issue of them not having any food, and hunger is an excellent motivator.

Jacob/Israel/whatever relents and sends the boy off to Egypt with his brothers to score some more grain. He implores them to, *"put some of the best products of the land in your packs as a gift – a little balm and a little honey, spices and myrrh, pistachio nuts and almonds" (Gen. 43: 11)*. Okay, I understand the spices and myrrh and balm, but the honey and nuts? You're buying food with, well, food. Okay yes, Egypt has grain for bread, but you *can* make flour out of almonds and indeed out of pistachios, if need be. He also packs double the silver to cover the cost of what was returned in the packs on the last trip, and to buy whatever they can for this trip, and off they go.

On arrival in Egypt, Joseph orders the steward to slaughter an animal and prepare a lunch for him and his brothers (although that fact isn't revealed, yet). The brothers are shitting themselves at this point and fear they'll be attacked and enslaved regarding the unexplained silver in their packs from the last trip, and worst of all having their donkeys taken from them. The horror! So they plead to Joseph's steward, saying they just wanted food the first trip, and that they found the silver, and were returning it all, with an equal extra amount to buy more food. The steward tells them it's cool, that God put the silver in their packs and that he had "received their silver". Messing with their heads, in other words. He then brought Simeon out to them, and took them to Joseph's house and did the whole feet-washing and donkey-feeding thing. Then Joseph rocked up, and they put their gifts before him and prostrated and all that rubbish while Joseph enquired about "their" aged old father back home. Then he spotted Benjamin and had to go away for a little wussy cry to himself. I mean really, the dude essentially controls Egypt and he acts like a little girly-man. Anyway, he comes back and serves lunch, and Benjamin's portion is five times the size of his brothers. Dunno why, just what it is, can't see how it's relevant in any way, shape or form. And the feast continued to the next chapter.

# Genesis 44: The old Silver Cup Inna Sack Trick

*"I have no religion, and at times I wish all religions at the bottom of the sea. He is a weak ruler who needs religion to uphold his government; it is as if he would catch his people in a trap."* –Mustafa Kemal Ataturk.

In this chapter, Joseph summons his steward and tells him to put the brothers' silver into the sacks just as before, but additionally to place Joseph's silver cup into Benjamin's sack (Gen. 44:2). This being done, the brothers are sent on their way the next morning on their respective donkeys. When they were well on their way, Joseph then tells the steward to give chase to them, and accuse them of theft, saying, *"Why have you repaid good with evil? Isn't this the cup my master drinks from and also uses for divination? This is a wicked thing you have done."* (Gen. 44:4, 44:5), and *"when he caught up with them, he repeated these words to them"* (Gen. 44:6).

It gets a little confusing from here, but essentially the brothers are like, "Dude, why would we do that, we even brought back the silver we found the first time, why would we start stealing shit now?" (44:8), before proclaiming that the person found with this cup will die, while the rest become my lord's slaves (44:9). Then the steward (presumably) is like, *"Alright, whoever is found to have the cup will be my slave, and the rest of you will be free from blame" (44:10).* The brothers quickly drop their respective grain sacks (44:11), and after searching them, they find the cup in Benjamin's sack (44:12), at which point they all tore their clothes (44:13).

So, we have a temporal paradox here. Gen. 44:6 clearly intimates that the silver cup was seen and its identity specifically questioned by the steward, HOWEVER, the cup was not actually found on the brothers until 44:12..! Did they have see-through sacks? If that was the case, it wasn't really necessary to search them. If the cup was hidden, then what silver cup were they referring to in the initial questioning in 44:6? Perhaps the cup originally belonged to Erwin Schrodinger, before he was allowed to lock cats up in boxes and gas them. Or after; Schrodinger was born in 1887 in Austria, so having his silver cup turn up in biblical Egypt with its quasi-existential powers intact is just as likely as the sequence of events in this bible verse, but whatever. My point is, the cup is both missing AND found at the same time and is in a state of existential flux, such that only opening the sack will determine the true state of the cup by collapsing the quantum probability wave-function through physical observation.

Anyway, they pack up all their donkeys and shit and return to the city and prostrate themselves before Joseph. Joseph then opines, *"What is this you have done? Don't you know that a man like me can find things out by divination?" (Gen. 44:15)*. Okay, ignoring the fact the Joseph set this whole sting up in the first place, the brothers should have picked up on the small matter of having the silver cup identified as the one Joseph "also uses for divination" in 44:5. To the brothers, the sixty-four shekel question should have been how Joseph could divine the theft without possession of the very cup needed to divine the theft; and if he had foreseen the theft, then surely steps should have been taken to avoid the theft in the first place, effectively dodging the Theft Prophesy.

Anyway, enter our old mate Judah, who pleas, *"What can we say? God has uncovered our servant's guilt. We are now my lord's slaves – we ourselves and the one who was found to have the cup." (Gen. 44:16)*. Joseph, however is all like, "Nah, how could I do that, I'll just take the one who had the cup as a slave and the rest of you can go back to your father." (44:17). Then Judah makes a man of himself and throws himself to Joseph's mercy, explaining all the shit that went on previously (44:18 – 44:34) and how the father will die if Benny isn't returned and how he offered surety of Benny's safety and so on, and ends his blubbering by offering himself as a slave in Benjamin's place. And that's the end of that chapter.

## Genesis 45: Joseph Blubbers Like A Little Girl

*"I looked up my family tree and found out I was the sap." –Rodney Dangerfield.*

Having heard Judah's impassioned plea for Benjamin, it seems Joseph can't hold onto his water any longer and orders everyone out of the room so that he can "reveal himself" to his brothers in privacy (45:1). Not that it mattered, of course: Joseph blubbered so loudly the whole household heard him. And so, Joseph revealed himself to his brothers and enquired about Jacob/Israel/whatever. He went on to say not to be distressed about selling him into Egyptian slavery, because it was God's will and that God put him in charge of all of Egypt so that he could save his family from famine and blah blah blah, reckons God made him the father to Pharaoh (oh my, that's drawing quite a long bow, Joe!), lord of Pharaoh's household and all of Egypt (no wonder he sent the Egyptians from the room!). He went on to ask that they return to Jacob/Israel/whatever and tell him to bring the whole tribe down to Egypt to live next to Joseph in the most fertile land, before dissolving into more weepiness and hugging and kissing his brothers, and then afterward discussed things with them.

Meanwhile, the Pharaoh had heard of Joseph's brothers coming to the city and he and his officials were pleased (lucky he didn't get wind of Joey claiming paternity over him, but whatever). So Pharaoh told Joseph to bring his fam to Egypt and provide for them and all that rubbish Joseph had already provided, in addition to the clothes and donkeys and hundreds of shekels and ten female donkeys (perhaps it was a longer journey than we supposed?), and implored them, *"Don't quarrel on the way!" (45:24)*. And thus ultimately, the old bastard Jacob/Israel/whatever was finally convinced of Joseph's continuing alive-ness and decided to shuffle on down and see him before he died. For a more detailed (read:boring) account, feel free to read the book, but it essentially boils down to that.

## Genesis 46: Jacob enters Egypt, More Mindnumbing Genealogy

*"The devil is in the detail." -Paulo Coelho.*

Oh hooray, another gripping and utterly fascinating chapter listing the sons of sons of sons and family relations and all things Genealogy, I hear none of you exclaim! Well, I don't really blame you, readers. I find it hard enough to get excited about my own genealogy, let alone trying to follow this lot, but as we've discovered throughout our travels of the bible, the devil really is in the detail, and not paying attention to what you're claiming can dissolve the credibility of your story quicker than a polystyrene cup in an acetone bath.

The chapter begins with Jacob/Israel/whatever packing up all his worldly shit and travelling off to Beersheba where he sets aside some time to wail at one of the altars there. That night (of course) God makes a miraculous appearance to Jacob/Israel/whatever and said, *"Jacob! Jacob!" (Gen. 46:2)*. I'm thinking it's been some time since the G-man has had dealings with him, because the whole bizarre idea of calling him Israel "from now on" seems to have slipped G's mind. Strike One.

Anyway, G tells Jacob/Israel/whatever not to be afraid to go to Egypt, for he will make him a great nation there. Additionally, *"I will go down to Egypt with you, and will surely bring you back again. And Joseph's own hand will close your eyes" (Gen. 46:4).* Nice to get an impromptu chaperone so late in the game, but Joseph's already set the ball rolling in getting his multi-named father into Egypt and onto the finest lands; God's just essentially tagging along for the ride and claiming the credit for everything; like the credit-stealing workmate who goes, "yeah I fixed that" after you've cleaned up the mess they caused in the first place through their incompetence. Strike Two.

And so begins the long, long list of what babies belong to what wife or sex slave. Mostly boring stuff, and I won't bother to regale you with its complete lack of fascinating-ness, except for one part concerning Rachel. As we all know, Jacob/Israel/whatever had only the two sons with Rachel, those being Joseph and Benjamin (*"The sons of Jacob's wife Rachel: Joseph and Benjamin (Gen. 46:19)*). And yet…. And yet! Just a couple of lines down, we read, *"These were the sons of Rachel who were born to Jacob – fourteen in all." (Gen. 46:22)*. So, is it TWO sons, or is it FOURTEEN? Is this another one of those ark things, where first it's two of every animal, and next thing you know it's sixteen of the buggers? That's a swing-and-a-miss if I've ever seen one! Steeeeeerike Three, you're outta there..!!!!

Shall we continue anyway? Why not, we're a patient bunch if you're still here reading me. So

Jacob/Israel/whatever sent Judah ahead to find Joseph in order to get directions to this Goshen place they were told to head for. Well, okay, fine, but isn't God currently accompanying Jacob/Israel/whatever to Egypt? Surely the Big G knows where Goshen is, and can provide adequate directions to the place? Mind you, since his promise of accompaniment (and safe passage) to and from Egypt, God has been curiously absent ever since. Bloody flaky deities, oh well. Anyway, Joseph came back with Judah and caught up with his old man and had another long cry about it (46:29).

Then Joseph tells his assembled family to claim that, if asked by the Pharaoh, they are shepherds and tenderers of livestock, which will grant them the right to settle in Goshen because apparently shepherds are detestable to Egyptians. Who knew…? I suppose it's true, then, what they say about shepherds and their flocks, when no other means of entertainment presents itself. No matter, that's how chapter 46 leaves us. Onward and upward, I suppose…

## Genesis 47: He who hath the food controls the world

*"Those that die by famine die by inches."* – *Matthew Henry.*

The first part is pretty boring, just an excerpt of what Jacob/Israel/whatever said when he fronted up to the Pharaoh and said what he was told to say, before blessing the Pharaoh (odd thing to do to a King, but whatever) and sodding off to do whatever it is old bastards do for fun in the middle east. And so Joseph and his tribe scored a sweet fertile plot in the Rameses district and they were all fed and watered, and lived it up on Egypt's largesse.

Except that there was no food, of course, there being a famine in the whole region (Gen.47:13). Joseph at the time was raking in all the money that was to be had, and gave it to the Pharaoh. Once that was gone, the people kept coming wanting food. Joseph told them that he would take livestock as payment for grain (Gen. 47:16). Once all the livestock had been sold off to purchase food, the people were reduced to selling themselves and their properties in exchange for food (Gen. 47:19- 47:20). And so *"The land became Pharaoh's, and Joseph reduced the people to servitude, from one end of Egypt to the other" (Gen. 47:20 – 47:21).*

Okay…. If a king rightly owns all his land, and a pharaoh is an Egyptian king, wouldn't that land belong to him in the first place? I'm pretty sure we haven't got to the stage of title deeds and whatnot, but rather Pharaoh as the divine ruler would "give" land to people to farm in exchange for a tribute (say, one fifth of the fruit of the land or some shit) which in essence is the first flat tax.

The priests, of course, did not starve. They had a regular allotment from the Pharaoh, and thus had sufficient food to not have to sell off any land. Ah, if only they didn't have this allotment, how the world could have been so much different today! But as we can see, religious piety has already established a fatal stranglehold on the weak-minded masses, such that a few select, otherwise-ordinary men are artificially elevated in status as to be near-divine, and given immense power and illusion of authority over other men, to which they have no right whatsoever. The Catholic Church is by far the biggest example of this corruption but there are so many others, particularly in the evangelical spheres of influence (the likes of Joel "Not Opening My Church Doors To Poor Wet People" Osteen springs to mind here), that makes a person wonder how the ordinary human creates such a high level of delusion within themselves. To make themselves so blind to their surroundings that they are, in every sense of the word, lambs to the slaughter.

Think about that for a moment. Evolution made humans' progenitors able to stand on two limbs instead of lumbering about on all four, giving us a tactical advantage over our predators. By standing upright, we were able to increase our visual range and thus to identify danger before it could get close enough to catch and eat us. What religion wants us to do – and you'll see it every Sunday, regular as clockwork – is to *close our eyes and bow our heads in prayer*. I find it elegantly symbolic; by doing this, we become blind and helpless to our predators. And while it might not be an actual sabre-tooth tiger on the prowl for some long pig anymore, this symbolic act of blind obeisance allows the wolves within our own species to prey on your weakness and strip you of your confidence, your self-esteem, your morals and especially your finances in one fell swoop. Perhaps it is for this very reason that evolution is so distasteful to organized religionism? How dare those evil, scientific Morlocks expose the sheep to their danger, and their scam job of fear! I feel George Carlin summed it up best of all when he said, "Religion rakes in billions of dollars, they pay no taxes, and they always need a little more." Furthermore, religion tries to "sell" mankind a place in some magnificent imaginary place called heaven (of which there is no proof) when you die, and there is no means of going back for a refund if their claims turn out to be false. It's the epitome of scams; no wonder they don't want men of Science barging in and screwing it up for them with their "logic" and their "reason" and their "evidence to the contrary"..! Notice I said "if" not "when" it turns out to be false. That is because we simply do not know what happens to our consciousness after we die. Nobody does, religion included; that's the point. Don't subscribe to the rhetoric: engage your curiosity and explore the possibilities of existence for yourself!

Anyway, back to the story. The famine is on, the people are starving, the land and all its wealth is in the hands of the Pharaoh, the people have been reduced to slavery, and all the food is in Joseph's control. Talk about holding all the aces! Now that the country is under a totalitarian regime, Joseph starts handing out seeds to the apprentice slaves to start growing food, one fifth of which will be kept by the Pharaoh, and the rest for feeding the nation. The masses, of course, thanked him for saving their lives, and went about their servitude. The Israelites, in the meantime, acquired the best land in the country near Goshen and multiplied and became fruitful and all that rubbish. Finally, old Jacob/Israel/whatever was nearing death's door and called Joseph over, told him to grab his nuts (that "hand under the thigh" thing) and made him swear not to bury him in Egypt.

Seriously, it would've been easier to just say "grab my nuts!" than try to hide it with all this hand-under-the-thigh business. Call it for what it is, I reckon...

## Genesis 48: Why won't you die already??! (and stop stealing my children)

*"Never knock on Death's Door: ring the doorbell and run, he hates that." – Matt Frewer.*

Some undefined time later, Joseph is told that his father Jacob/Israel/whatever is ill; and so he heads off to see the old bugger before he kicks the bucket. Perhaps. Because on his arrival, Jacob/Israel/whatever rallies his strength and sits up in bed (48:2). So anyway, because he's so bloody old and blind and mostly senile, Jacob/Israel/whatever starts regaling Joseph of the good ol' days when he and G were kickin' it in Luz, and about how he was going to be fruitful and all that other rubbish. Good times for Jizzy. Then he turns around and says, *"Your two sons born to you in Egypt before I came to you here will be reckoned as mine"* (Gen. 48:5).

Okay, you crazy old bugger, you're about to die and you're claiming ownership of two more kids, who already have a father, your own son. Talk about short-term arrangements! You really have to wonder, though, what's going on in Jacob/Israel/whatever's head to be doing this now. Let's read on and see where he's going with this.

So now he's rabbiting on about having to bury Rachel on the side of the road, and then for some reason Joseph's two rugrats have been brought into the conversation; because when

Jacob/Israel/whatever, *"saw the sons of Joseph he said, 'Who are these?'" (Gen. 48:8)*. Joseph, of course, replying that they were the sons "God has given me here." Well, no, they're the offspring you have because you had intercourse with a female, but hey, whatever these people want to believe. Jacob/Israel/whatever says to bring them to him so that he could bless them. And because the old bugger's eyes were failing he brought them closer and they all got a hug and a smooch. Awww...

Then Jacob/Israel/whatever (I'll be *so* glad when he dies and I don't have to keep typing that anymore!) says, *"I never expected to see your face again, but now God has allowed me to see your children too." (Gen. 48:11)*. Wait, I thought the old bugger's eyes were failing? Well, perhaps the waterworks from the hugging and smooching created a temporary lens effect that helped him to focus one last time, who knows? Mere supposition and semantics, moving on. Then Joseph *"removed them from Israel's knees and bowed down with his face on the ground (48:12)*. So, is Jacob/Israel/whatever in bed, or sitting on a chair? The last we read, he'd rallied his strength and sat up in his bed (48:2); it would be grossly irresponsible of anyone to then plonk two boisterous lads onto the knees of a 147-year-old man (as the bible claims was his age at the time of his death). Sure, you might plonk them down *next to* the old bugger if need me, but you wouldn't be putting any sort of direct pressure on old bones, trust me on this. So inconsiderate of people back then.

So comes the blessing. Joseph brings his brats in so that his father can bestow his blessings, and Jacob/Israel/whatever unexpectedly crosses his arms and blesses them in reverse, the younger son with his right hand and the older with his left, in contravention with local custom, and blessed Joseph as well, saying, *"May the God who blessed (blah blah blah, read it yourself), may he bless these boys. May they be called by my name and names of my fathers Abraham and Isaac, and may they increase greatly on the earth."* (Gen. 48:16). So, not just a blessing, but yet another name-change or three; just who gets what name is up for debate, I suppose, but honestly, it's enough to give a historical genealogist an apoplexy. Anyway, Joseph is pissed off that the old bugger has blessed the kids arse-about, and tries to correct the mistake. Jacob/Israel/whatever refuses, though, and says that, although both boys will be great, the younger one will be greater and become a group of nations; the usual spiel. Then he says, *"In your name will Israel pronounce this blessing: may God make you like Ephraim and Manasseh."* (Gen. 48:20). Ugh… they're *already* Ephraim and Manasseh you old twit, asinine renaming ritual notwithstanding; they don't *have* to be made that way, least of all by appealing some deity who got false credit for giving them to Joseph in the first place!

Then Jacob/Israel/whatever said, *"I am about to die* (thank God for that, if nothing else!), *but God will be with you and take you back to the land of our fathers." (Gen. 48:21)*. Then he bequeaths Joseph with one more plot of land than the rest of his brothers, which was that ridge he took from the Amorites with his sword and bow. Which, after some extensive Google searching, is a reference to Chapter 34, when Jacob's sons contrived to get the Shechemites to circumcise themselves before brutally slaughtering the lot of them while they were still recovering from their self-inflicted wounds, although it doesn't mention Amorites anywhere in what we've covered. Ah, but when did the bible ever have to make sense, eh..? Thankfully, we haven't far to go, at least as far as Genesis is concerned.

## Genesis 49: FINALLY – but not before a little Soothsaying...

*"Death may be the greatest of all human blessings."*
*–Socrates.*

As the ultra-annoying guy drones at us relentlessly on commercial television, "But wait, there's more..!!" Jacob/Israel/whatever still has some kick in him yet, for he gathers his sons around him and prepares to tell them what will happen in the days to come (Gen. 49:1). Side note: have you ever noticed how daughters are rarely, if ever, considered in this book other than for convenient procreation? With all these sons being born with hardly any mention of daughters, one can only assume that the females had all the rights and privileges of breeding-stock, if they were lucky. Secondly, there seems to be a lot of soothsaying and fortune-telling going on that, if I'm not mistaken, modern religion considers as dealing in dark matters, even going so far as to call it devil-worship. How many women were burned at the stake and drowned and tortured and executed for being proclaimed a witch, at the behest (and blessing) of the church? Being a "witch" of course meaning anything from having a facial wart or wearing a funny hat, to having a heart-warming cackle around their cooking pot. It's amusing how modern Christians today (particularly women) will proclaim the eternal love of their god for all of his creation, and yet declaim fortune-telling as demon-worship and ignoring the slaughter of millions of innocent women in their god's name. A logical, rational perspective, as I have always said, needs to be applied to this book for its own good, before we end up brainwashed into believing two contradictory things to be true at the same time. DOUBLEPLUSUNGOOD for anyone who falls into that trap.

Gen. 49:2 illustrates this perfectly: *"Assemble and listen, sons of Jacob; listen to your father Israel."* Seriously, just choose a name and be done with it, dude. Thankfully he is knocking on heaven's door so we won't have to put up with his nonsense for too much longer. First cab off the rank is Reuben, whom Jacob/Israel/whatever describes as *"excelling in honour"*, yet tells him that he will no longer excel because he *"went up onto your father's bed, onto my couch, and defiled it." (49:4)*. This, of course, being a reference to Reuben getting it on with his father's concubine Bilbah/Bilhah/whatever (nice how he calls his wives and concubines "couches", isn't it, like they have no more importance or significance than household furniture).

Then come the brothers Simeon and Levi, who put an entire city to death in anger and even worse, *"hamstrung oxen as they pleased,"* and he vowed to *"scatter them in Jacob and disperse them in Israel!" (Gen. 49:7).* I was not aware of any countries called Jacob, although as we know there is an Israel floating about over there. Seems an exceedingly odd thing to say, but we have to remember he's 147 years old and his faculties have all but deserted him. Perhaps back then they were naming countries after their fathers or their goats or whatever, so perhaps there's something in it. Either way, he contrives to separate the pair for their own good. Well, best of luck to you, old man.

Judah gets a whole bunch of praise from the old bugger, calls him a lion, and proclaims some shit about donkeys tied to vines and washing clothes in the blood of grapes, etc. Basically all good stuff, so obviously Jacob/Israel/whatever never discovered that it was Judah who sold Joseph off into Egyptian slavery in the first place. Or else he did, but then saw the result of that and thought, "Eh.. nice bit of precognition that, we'll just let that one slide, the ends justify the means and all that…"

Another son, Zebulun scored some choice seaside land for shipping concerns, while Issachar gets called a rawboned donkey. Dan gets a judiciary position in Israel, comparing him to, *"a snake by the roadside, a viper along the path, that bites the horse's heels so that its rider stumbles backwards." (Gen. 49:17).* So perhaps just a lawyer, then (insert any number of Jewish lawyer jokes here).

Gad is promised an attack by raiders, but Gad will then attack them at their heels; whatever. Asher is promised a chef's position in some royal house, then *"Naphtali is a doe set free that bears beautiful fawns." (Gen. 49:21)*. Nice, calling your son a girl in front of his brothers like that. Joseph is vaunted as the rock-star of the children (no surprises there), calling him a vine that grows over the wall and what not, and claiming credit for his success purely by being his father and throwing in an Honourable Mention to God (Jacob/Israel/whatever's god, that is) in Joseph's successes, naming him prince among his brothers (good grief, if they sold him off into slavery for the wheat sheaf dream, imagine what they're going to do to him now!). Finally, he calls Benjamin a ravenous wolf who shares his plunder. A bit of an anticlimax, but meh.

### The Final, Actual, Honest-for-True Death of Jacob/Israel/Whatever. Honestly..!

So finally, after all the promises of it happening, the old bugger's time was nigh. He claimed the darkness was encroaching, and asked them to *"Bury me with my fathers in the cave in the field of Ephron the Hittite" (Gen. 49:29)*, there to be buried with Crazy Old Abe and Sarah, with Isaac and Rebekah, and with his first wife Leah.

And having said this, crawled back into bed and finally died.

Huzzah!

Odd choice that, although having a lifelong preference for the younger sister Rachel, he chose to be buried next to Leah. You would've thought he'd opt for the roadside burial to be next to Rachel, but I dunno, perhaps he had an attack of conscience on the doorstep to oblivion and went for the safer option, thinking that maybe he'd earn some brownie points with God should he have to answer for his actions now that he's in God's domain now. Do we know? Not at all. Do we care? Not a whit. All I know for sure is that, beyond a passing reference, I no longer have to deal with his infernally irritating naming issues, and *that* is worth celebrating.

## Genesis 50: Business as Usual

*"The entrepreneur always searches for change, responds to it, and exploits it as an opportunity." – Peter Drucker.*

So Jacob/Israel/whatever finally – finally! – dies, and Joseph threw himself onto his father and wept over him and whatnot. He then directed his physicians to embalm his father, and so they did, *"taking a full forty days, for that was the time required for embalming." (Gen. 50:3).* And so we herald perhaps the first Jewish mummy known to exist. After this process, Joseph throws himself before Pharaoh's court and seeks permission to fulfil his father's wishes to be buried in the cave next to his kin, which is agreed to (Gen. 50:6), and thus he took his family and an escort of Pharaoh's officials, dignitaries, and so forth to the cave where they interred the old bugger. There's some unrelated stuff about threshing floors going into mourning, but mainly it is described for all intents and purposes as a state funeral-slash-public holiday, fly-the-flags-at-half-mast sort of occasion.

### Joseph's Brothers – Saving their Skins

It was at the moment of their father's passing that the rest of Joseph's brothers got to thinking, and said amongst themselves, *"What if Joseph holds a grudge and pays us back for all the wrongs we did to him?" (Gen. 50:15).* So they conspired to send word to Joseph, saying, *"Your father left these instructions before he died: 'This is what you are to say to Joseph: I ask you to forgive your brothers their sins and the wrongs they committed in treating you so badly.' Now please forgive the sins of the servants of the God of your father." (Gen. 50:16 – 50:17).* Clever, cunning sausages, hitting Joseph in the father like that. Firstly, there's no way to actually verify that Jacob/Israel/whatever had said such a thing, but also timing their request when Joseph is weakest in his mourning (him being a sooky-la-la at the best of times). Besides, Joseph should have realized that no such behest was given, and that the sins of the brothers was unknown to their father, otherwise he would not have praised Judah as much as he did despite him selling Joseph into slavery in the first place. It would be no different to me rocking up to the wake and saying, "Hey Joey, your father said to me before he died to gimme 3,000 sheckels and that nice plot of land near the only permanent source of water." You'd smell a rat if you were in his sandals, dear readers, and by rights Joseph should have too.

But we know what a sook Joseph is, so we know without even consulting the book that he a) cries; and b) forgives his brothers. The brothers properly abase themselves before Joseph of course, who acknowledges their sins, but that it was okay because it all turned out in the end for him and it was God's plan for it to happen that way, to save all the people from the famine and all the rest of that rot, and then promises to provide for them and all of their children. I tell you, if there really is a sucker born every minute, Joseph is the jawbreaker of them all.

## The Death of Jawbreaker – er, Joseph

So Joseph ended up staying in Egypt and living to be 110 years old, and he had children put on his knees just like his father did, and so on and so forth. And on his deathbed, he said to his brothers, *"I am about to die. But God will surely come to your aid and take you up out of this land to the land he promised on oath to Abraham, Isaac and Jacob." (Gen. 50:24)*. A pretty long time for G-man to come good on his promises, if you ask me. Promised to Crazy Old Abe of the ark, this land seems to have been in proprietorial flux for such an insanely long time that you'd think these guys would have just upped and took it by force by now. They've already proven their ability to destroy entire cities (albeit by deception), and the population's general unwillingness to learn from the mistakes of others suggests that a similar tactic would work again, if only they could convince the entire world to circumcise (and therefore, incapacitate) themselves at their request. Show them a nice bit of naked female leg, get 'em to slice up their junk, then hack off their bonces before they can say, "Ow." Foolproof, I say.

Then, making the Israelites swear to carry his bones from the place when (if) it did happen, he died. They embalmed him, and then put him in a coffin in Egypt. And that, dear readers, is the end of Genesis as we know it.

## Genesis: The Summary

*"If you want a happy ending, that depends, of course, on where you stop your story." –Orson Welles.*

So what can we take away from this analysis of the bible, my dear readers?

I suppose it depends on how you read the book, of course. Throughout our journey through Genesis, I have been asking you to open your minds and not listen blindly to anything anyone tells you in a book, and that includes this book. Sure, I've expressed my opinion on countless occasions on various glaring inconsistencies, but then that's my right, it's my bloody book after all. You don't have to agree with what I've said, and I'm certainly open to the possibility that I could be horribly wrong about the lot of it, but logic and reason would suggest otherwise. The logical, physical facts of our universe have been translated as accurately as possible, but even so I implore you, the reader, to check these things out for yourself. My calculations could most certainly be off, but not by so very much that it would affect the outcome. My point is, open your minds, cast aside the blinkers that society (and religion in particular) has put on your thinking, and explore every possibility, for *and* against, and make your own judgment forged through objective research and rational conclusions!

If I had to put money on whether religion or science has the right of how we came to being, the safe money would be on science all the way, but that's not to say that there's no elements of truth in the bible either; it's just been obscured over the years, misinterpreted, misunderstood through lack of knowledge and experience and relayed like a 6,000 year old game of Chinese Whispers. "Noah built an ark and rescued the animals" turns into "Noah built an ark potato jacket llama rescued the dining room chairs with olive tree prints on them", purely because that's how verbal recitation works. Facts get distorted, eyewitness accounts are unreliable, and without an impartial medium to record these things for eternity, the truth of the matter may never be known.

So what about our major players? Well, there's the biggest player of them all, the G-man. Supposed to be all-wise, all-seeing, all-knowing, the alpha and omega of our entire existence, yet what do we make of the ... man? Deity? Alien? What, exactly, is he? The creator of man? The standard of moral behaviour towards which we must ever strive? Personally speaking, I'll wait for a better role model. God is, gauging by the events in his own book, an egotistic, vengeful, unforgiving, sadistic, forgetful, utterly corrupt individual. As described in Bruce Almighty, he is the proverbial bully with a magnifying glass, and we are the ants, assuming Genesis has any basis in fact whatsoever. We know he is not infallible, or the Great Flood would never have occurred, to attempt to erase his mistakes. We know he has trouble keeping track of what he does, because God contradicts himself in several places and repeats himself in others. We know that he is sadistic and enjoys watching others dance through his twisted hoops, or circumcision would never have been thought of (and you'd have to be a pretty sick and twisted motherfucker to first conceive such a practice, and then convince people to actually do it to themselves). We know he doesn't take threats to his authority very well, as evidenced by both the Flood and the Tower of Babel, making him megalomaniacal and power-hungry. In short, God is the quintessential (and original) psychopath.

Then we have Adam and Eve: poor buggers never really stood a chance, did they, on the Dawn of Consciousness and not a jot of life experience to help them navigate the pitfalls of dealing with a psychotic creator. Tried their best, but ultimately caught the rough end of the stick.

Noah: Ah, Noah. Crazy old bastard, enjoyed building boats and had an unhealthy obsession with animals. The holder of the inaugural "You Had One Job" meme. The first one to be sent chasing his tail for God's personal amusement, the cryptococcal meningitis and alcoholism eventually got the better of him.

Abram/Abraham: Crazy ol' Abe, the first to conspire with God to commit real estate fraud, the first (well, first recorded) instance of extramarital sex, and the first to grab his penis and hack the tip off it with a sharp object. We can all learn from Abe.

Abe's Descendants: Explicitly the line of Isaac, Jacob/Israel/whatever and so on. But not Esau. If this part of the saga has taught us anything, is that boring family lines do *not* make for a good storyline. Nay, the bloodlines with the most drama, the most dysfunction, the most sinful amorality and foul bloody murder, the more engrossing the story. Esau? Who's he? Jacob's brother, who traded his birthright for a mess of pottage. That's his one and only contribution, along with one chapter outlining his offspring, and that's pretty much it. Very boring, yes, but ultimately saner and far more inherently moral. How different the world would be today if the bible followed the adventures (or lack thereof) of Esau and his descendants? "He got up, never did a bad thing to anyone, loved his wife unconditionally and took no others, worked hard and honestly, was kind to his kids, and died. Rinse and repeat." Just imagine if everyone in the world adopted that philosophy! Where would we be as a species, without the pettiness and avarice that so plagues our efforts at self-betterment. We could easily have conquered the stars by now (if only, perhaps, the ones in our immediate solar system). With such a philosophy towards the common benefit of all mankind, we could be so utterly unified as a species that the world, nay the universe would be laid open before us, our reach limited only by the boundaries of reality itself. There would be no hunger, no poverty, no disease, no wars. We could, literally, be living the Star Trek dream envisioned by Gene Roddenberry all those years ago. And how wonderful would that be?

Instead, the bible has given us the Isaac version of things, and religious institutions have cemented it into our culture to be the go-to book for our moral guidance. And what does that guidance teach us? That it's okay to screw over your starving brother for material gain. To pose as that same brother to steal his blessings. To steal from your employer. To steal from your father and then lie about it when confronted. To sell your own brother into slavery if you don't like his smack talk. To wheedle, to deceive, to condemn, to murder, to rape, to be incestuous, to defraud, to set traps for others, and to deflect the blame if you're caught out. This book – this bible – is supposed to be our guide to being better people, yet if you want to shoe-horn the book into that description, it could only be by saying it's a guide to what NOT to do. Yet curiously, those most obsessed with the bible tend to follow its teachings to the letter, and not for the good, instead using it as an excuse behave badly towards others and to avoid responsibility for their actions when they're brought to account for them. How utterly deplorable. Surely we are evolved enough to be able to hold ourselves to a higher standard of ethics and behaviour? I hope so, but unless and until we free ourselves from the stranglehold of guilt organized Religionism has on our hearts and minds, progress will be slow at best.

## CONCLUSION

So here we are, readers, at the end of my first book. I hope you enjoyed your journey with me, and that I've made a rather unpalatable book a little bit more bearable, if not amusing. The same goes for the bible... (Insert drum fill here).

Now, as promised, I have compiled a handy go-to, ready-reference guide thingy for when those Sunday-spawned God-botherers come darkening your door when all you want is to catch some extra sleep. A few well-placed counter-arguments should drive them away, never to return. Who knows, perhaps with enough persuasion they could be convinced to see the error of their ways and perhaps they will broaden their horizons beyond their blinkered, religious existence. Well, one step at a time, yeah..?

Bear in mind that this book has only concerned itself with Genesis, being the very first part of the bible and only the tip of a very convoluted and confusing iceberg. As a result, the most common response you will get when you counter any arguments with door-bashing god-botherers is, "Oh, but that's the Old Testament, we don't subscribe to that; we follow the New Testament," or any number of other fictitious, cherry-picked parts they choose to believe in. That being the case, ask them why. Ask them, is the God of the Old Testament and Genesis not the same God of the New Testament? Are you saying there's more than one God? Has God changed his tune since the Old Testament? If so, what made him change his attitude towards Mankind? It can't have been Mankind, we're mere mortals; how could we dare presume to change the personality and behaviour of a God, particularly the vengeful, smiting God of Genesis? Failure to answer these questions to your satisfaction will allow you to assert that the God of Old and New is one and the same God, and therefore your argument is a valid one. Then stand back a little bit and watch them squirm in the juices of their doubt.

It is my intention to, eventually, work my way through the entire bible, but that is a VERY long journey and I am a very slow writer. In the meantime, I believe these arguments should work regardless of what they try to throw at your doorstep.

| **IF THEY USE:** | **COUNTER WITH:** | **REF**. |
|---|---|---|
| God created the universe | So where was God living before that? | 1:1 |
| God created everything | Do you think he enjoyed working in the dark? | 1:1 |
| | So why did he need Adam's rib to create Eve? | 2:21 |

|   |   |   |
|---|---|---|
|   | Why create so much universe just for two people? |   |
| Cain and Abel | Where did Cain's wife come from? | 4:16 |
|   | What was her name? Where was Nod, and who called it that? |   |
| Anything about the Ark | So was it 2 or 16 of each animal? | 6:19 |
|   | How did he save two of each fish and drown the rest? | 7:2 |
|   | Why did Noah save the animals only to burn them afterward? |   |
| Anything about circumcision | What sort of God justifies self-mutilation? | 17 |
|   | What's the deal with the name changes? | 17:5 |
| Anything about Onanism and masturbation | It's about birth control, not self-pleasure. | 38:9 |
|   | Onan was sleeping with his brother's wife, not wanking; get it right. |   |

If the God Squad haven't run from your door by now, start quoting from this book directly and they should never bother you again. You're welcome…!

**FINAL THOUGHTS**

It is my fervent hope that all of you, my dear readers, find they are descended from Esau, should the fables have any element of truth in them. The other mob was just too damned nasty;

There are a lot of people who will hate my interpretation of Genesis, proclaiming that I've "missed the point," and, "It's not meant to be taken like that," and so on and so forth. For those misguided individuals, hey: it's my book, my interpretations, and I didn't force you to read it. Therefore, sod off and don't tell me what to think;

If there's nothing else you take away from this book, remember one thing: NOBODY knows what happens to you after death, not even religion. You don't know until you get there. Why spend all your life being, say, Christian, when you should have been a Muslim? Or a Hindu? Or any other of the 4,200 religions currently being worshipped on this planet? What will you do then, eh? Seriously, just spend the rest of your life being the best person you can possibly be to others, and let your life speak for itself.

If you have enjoyed reading this irreverent but thought-provoking treatise, please feel free to let your friends and well-wishers know about your reading experience. It is available in paperback as well as in eBook format worldwide. Seriously though, the more people we can rescue from the clutches of Religionism, the sooner our species has a chance to evolve for the better, and the sooner we can become the enlightened civilization we all know we should be by now; hopefully, before the next big ball of ice floats down and blasts us back into the stone-age.

Er, and that's it, really. Thanks for reading!

www.ingramcontent.com/pod-product-compliance
Lightning Source LLC
Chambersburg PA
CBHW031948080426
42735CB00007B/304